Hunting Old Snowbeard's Gold

Searches for and Seekers of the Lost Dutchman Gold Mine

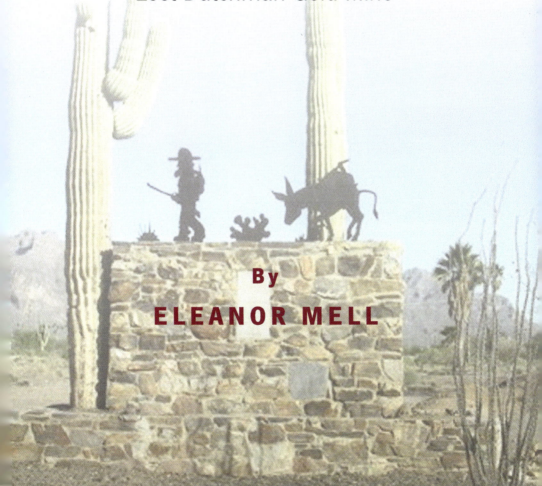

By
ELEANOR MELL

Copyright © 2012 Eleanor Mell
All rights reserved.

ISBN: 1469950200
ISBN 13: 9781469950204

Library of Congress Control Number: 2012904227
CreateSpace, North Charleston, SC

DEDICATION

To my husband Bob, without you, this book would not have happened. Thank you for your patience, support, chauffeuring, and love.

CONTENTS

Acknowledgements		vii
1	The Mystery	1
2	Old Snowbeard	5
3	A Good Waltz	11
4	A Dying Waltz	17
5	Newspapers And Legends	23
6	Dutchman Hunters Abound	29
7	Feuding On The Needle	39
8	Modern Hunters	45
9	End Of A Century	51
10	The Next Century	57
Things As They Happened		63
List Of Further Exploring		75
Bibliography		77
Index		83

ACKNOWLEDGMENTS

To the people of the: Arizona Historical Society, Goldfield Ghost Town and Museum, Lost Dutchman State Park, Pinal County Historical Society and Museum, Sharlot Hall Museum, and Superstition Mountain Historical Society and Museum—thank you for your assistance and information.

To Tom Kollenborn, whom I consider the "Historian of the Superstitions", thank you for your works.

To Ron Feldman and John Wilburn, a special thanks for your time and words. I enjoyed talking with you.

Finally, to all Dutchman Hunters, past, present and future, I appreciate the chance to partake in the adventure.

1

THE MYSTERY

Back in 1884, a man walked into a general store along the trail between Phoenix and Tucson, Arizona. He was there to get some flour for his biscuits, salted meat for when he couldn't find game, coffee for his mornings and bullets for his gun. He gathered his supplies and paid for them with gold. A young woman there that day told Tom Kollenborn, a local historian, that the old man had a face "parched dry from the desert sun and as hard as leather. His beard was almost snow-white and somewhat stained by tobacco below his chin. His hands were coarse and calloused revealing many decades of hard work."

The man was Jacob Waltz, "Old Snowbeard" to some and "The Dutchman" to others.

What stood out was how the old man paid for his supplies. He had a "small cowhide poke. He loosened the strings and poured on to the counter yellow gold in a matrix of white quartz. After gathering his supplies he left as quietly as he came."

The gold ore he used was some of the richest ever seen and soon to start a mystery that still lives today, over decades after his death.

Waltz's buying food with gold ore is not as odd as it sounds. In 1884, the United States currency consisted of gold and silver certificates along with gold, silver or copper coins. Anyone could take a gold certificate or note and exchange it at the local Federal Reserve Bank for the real thing. The silver notes worked the same way. Although gold notes appeared first in 1863, the silver notes became the popular paper money when they came out in 1878. Back then, the United States Treasury could only issue the notes for equal amounts of gold and silver held within their vaults.

Silver coins were the favored change. In the late 1800s, a pocket full could easily become too heavy to handle. The coins had to include a specific amount of the precious metal. A silver dollar had to contain 371.25 grains of pure silver. A person living along the Atlantic coast had easy access to the money; they were in the heart of America. What about the pioneer or prospector living way out West?

A few of the prospectors did have some of the gold- and silver-backed notes. They got the money by selling their ore to the United States Mint either in San Francisco, California, or to stagecoach drivers and general store managers who used assaying tools. After weighing and testing the ore for its gold or silver value, the Assayer would fix a price and buy the ore. Other miners in remote areas simply turned their ore over in return for supplies. Some miners just used their claims to trade for supplies. So with all the ways of buying supplies, a prospector spilling gold ore onto a counter was not at all odd.

What was odd was the type of gold ore Old Snowbeard had, some of the richest ever seen. Raw ore is a mixture, or rather, matrix of rocks, dirt and minerals taken from the earth. The amount of gold it contains and the grade or purity of the gold tells how rich the ore is. Old Snowbeard's gold was tiny nuggets, small flakes and short wires of free gold in a bed of white quartz. Free gold means that instead of smelting, smashing the ore will free the gold from its matrix. It also means Waltz's ore had more gold than quartz.

Free gold is rare and so is pure gold. Waltz's gold was twenty-four karats, the highest grade. Quite a rare thing, ore so full of pure gold that it was free for the mining. The only known gold mine in Arizona with such rich ore is the Vulture Mine, near Wickenburg. The Vulture Mine was the source of some of the richest gold ore in the world. Yet, Waltz hunted gold in the Superstition Wilderness, not the Wickenburg area northwest of Phoenix.

The Superstition Mountain Range, or simply the Superstitions are the heart of the almost 187 square miles of desert wilderness. This is the area in which Waltz hunted gold. People saw Waltz in the area east of Phoenix, south of Tortilla Flat, west of Globe and north of Florence, Arizona. In the late 1800s, there were plenty of gold strikes in the area too. The Mammoth Mine, the Mormon Stope and the Bulldog Mine are some of the larger strikes. Some of the smaller strikes had names like the Black King, Mother Hubbard and Tom Thumb. But of all the gold mines in and around the Superstitions, none ever showed ore as rich as Old Snowbeard's.

Where did Old Snowbeard get his gold? No one knows for sure. Old Snowbeard kept his gold mine a secret all his life. Where the gold came from became a mystery the day Old Snowbeard died, a mystery still unsolved after decades of searching. How could anyone keep one of the richest gold mines in the world a secret? Perhaps exploring the man's past will reveal the answer.

2

OLD SNOWBEARD

Over the years, people have wondered why Old Snowbeard kept his gold mine a secret. Rumor has it that Waltz killed a group of Mexican miners, stole their gold and kept the mine a secret to hide his crime. Others say Waltz found his mine in the Superstitions and kept quiet to prevent a gold rush to the area. People even think Waltz and his gold are a myth, that they never existed. Records show that Old Snowbeard lived and witnesses state he struck it rich in the Superstition Wilderness of Arizona.

Oberschwandorf, Württemberg, a small village near Germany's Black Forest, has a register showing the birth of

Waltz in 1810. Some say Waltz left the village to go to work in his cousin's animal skin tannery in New Jersey. Most agree Waltz came to America in 1839, landing in either New York or Baltimore, Maryland. There are no files to show where and when he landed.

Waltz made his way down south where at least one person believes he fought in the Civil War as a Confederate. Others believe Waltz joined the first gold rushes of America. North Carolina had a gold rush in 1826 and Northern Georgia in 1828. Whatever the reason, Waltz moved to Mississippi. He signed a Letter of Intention to become a citizen of the United States in the Adams County Courthouse, Natchez, Mississippi, on September 12, 1848.

No one knows for sure what Waltz did during the next twelve years, but in 1860, he showed up in California. A census of the Azusa Township, Los Angeles County, California, has his name. The entry reads, "Jacob Walls, age 50, place of birth, Germany."

Although the last name is wrong, historians agree that this was Waltz working with five other hired hands at a gold mine.

While in California, Waltz became a citizen of the United States on July 19, 1861. Naturalization papers from the First District Court of Los Angeles County, California prove this fact. As a citizen of the United States, Waltz could now file gold mining claims. Maybe that is why he moved on to the Arizona Territory, to find his own gold mine and file a claim.

On September 21, 1863, Old Snowbeard legally became a prospector. He signed the first of three mining claims in Prescott, Arizona. In May of 1864, a Special Territorial Census taken by the Prescott Postmaster confirmed Old Snowbeard's new status. Entry number 1008 reads:

> Name: Jacob Waltz.
> Comment: Two years in the Territory, age 54, a native of Germany.
> Occupation: Miner.

Old Snowbeard stayed in Prescott from about 1862 to 1865, working three mining claims. The claims were the Gross Lode in 1863, Big Rebel in 1864, and General Grant Lode in 1865. No one knows how much gold

Waltz dug up, but a few think he stored a fortune in the Superstitions. They also say that when his last claim panned out, no more gold, Waltz moved to Phoenix to retire and live off his cache.

Waltz did move to Phoenix by the Spring of 1868. He bought 160 acres of land north of the Salt River. When he built a house and a chicken coop, Waltz showed he planned to stay in Phoenix.

Old Snowbeard made the nearly 107 mile trek from Prescott south to Phoenix at the age of fifty-eight. Thought of as an old man in those days, he probably wanted to stop roaming. Within ten years, Waltz showed signs of caring about his final years. On August 8, 1878, Waltz signed his land, some grain, two horses, his chickens and $50 cash to his neighbor Andrew Starar. In return, Starar agreed to let Waltz stay on his ranch and take care of him if he got sick.

Other facts about Old Snowbeard during his last years show that he settled in Phoenix. The Federal Census, dated August 30, 1870, for the Territory of Arizona, Yavapai County, lists him as a sixty-year-old farmer. Waltz proved to be a good citizen of his new country as well. He paid taxes in 1875 and 1877, and registered to vote in 1876, 1882 and 1886.

Waltz even made the newspapers. The *Arizona Gazette* of Wednesday, June 18, 1884, reported that:

> About 10 o'clock this morning word was received that a Mexican by the name of Pedro Ortega had been murdered, at the house of Jacob Waltz, one mile southeast of this city ... Ortega was shot and killed by a shotgun belonging to Jacob Waltz ...

Waltz claimed that someone else used his shotgun to kill Ortega. He told the Sheriff that Ortega fought with another of his hired hands; Ortega did the shooting. Waltz said he heard a shotgun blast, ran around the side of the house and found Ortega dead. Since the other man ran off, the Sheriff figured he was guilty of the crime and had no reason to doubt Waltz. The Sheriff closed the case. Gossip has it that Waltz was the shooter and bribed the Sheriff so he could get away with murder.

When Old Snowbeard signed up to vote in 1876, he said the only thing he owned was a horse. He must have put that horse to good use. From 1873 to 1876, people saw Waltz roaming the Superstitions and selling gold in Florence, Arizona. One of his neighbors, Johnny Grijalva, told an *Arizona Republic* newspaper reporter that, "He [Waltz] would take to the hills along about the first of November and return about the middle of March or the first days of April."

Old Snowbeard took a chance hunting gold on his own. Besides Apaches, Waltz had to protect himself from fellow prospectors. Back then, a man could travel for days without seeing another soul. Between towns and Army forts, travelers had to fend for themselves in the sandy, prickly, barren wilderness.

Because of the lack of people, greed for gold often led a person of low morale-values to kill a miner for a claim. They called these murderers claim jumpers. Waltz met one once.

Waltz filed an Affidavit of Claim Jumping in Pinal County on March 21, 1872. The Affidavit states that Waltz warned the man in front of witnesses to "get off his property and stay off."

The man could have been Richard "Dick" Holmes. Holmes knew Waltz had a source of gold somewhere in the Superstitions. Holmes admitted watching Waltz, following him as he left under the cover of darkness. Holmes even knew that Old Snowbeard would take a roundabout way into the Superstitions, sometimes camping for several days watching for anyone following him. Although the Affidavit does not name Holmes as the claim jumper, Holmes did show signs of being one.

Claim jumpers. Angry Apaches. These were not the only people Old Snowbeard knew—he did have a few friends. Besides his neighbors, Waltz was good friends with two other Germans, Julia Thomas and Rhinehart "Reiney" Petrasch. He met them when selling fresh eggs from his chickens. Thomas needed eggs for baking sweets that she sold from her store in Phoenix. Old Snowbeard would often stay for dinner. They were such good friends that Waltz gave Thomas about $500 in gold to pay her bills. Thomas had the chance to return the favor when Old Snowbeard was in over his head, too—only this time it was water.

On February 19, 1891, Phoenix endured a tragic flood. When the rains got too much for the Salt River to handle, it let loose its fury and tried to wash part of Phoenix away—including Old Snowbeard. Waltz's neighbor, Eugenio Grijalva, said that when he saw Waltz in a tree next to his flooded burro corral, he rode fast into town to find the Sheriff. The Sheriff quickly grabbed a deputy and seized a man with a wagon, rushing to Waltz's ranch to save him. Holmes' son later claimed that his father was the man with the wagon.

Thomas had a different story. She said she sent Reiney to check on their friend the night of the flood. Reiney found Waltz sitting in bed soaked and freezing. Waltz had tried to save his chickens by putting them on top of the coop. Because Waltz could not stop shaking, Reiney helped him onto his horse and took him back to town. Thomas said Reiney saved Waltz.

No matter who saved him, Waltz ended up in the one-room adobe behind Thomas' shop the day after the flood. All Waltz had were the clothes on his back. Perhaps that is why Waltz told Thomas about the gold ore he hid under the fireplace at his ranch. When the floodwaters faded, Thomas sent Reiney to fetch the gold. Reiney came back from the ranch with enough gold ore to fill a candlestick box. Thomas placed the box under Waltz's bed.

Julia Thomas tried to nurse Old Snowbeard back to health, but his chills turned into pneumonia. Then, before sunrise on October 25, 1891, Waltz had trouble breathing. Thomas knew she had to get the doctor, but she did not want to leave her friend alone. Thomas yelled for Reiney to come and sit with Waltz. When she got no response, Thomas asked a stranger passing by on his way to the livery stable to keep Waltz company. The stranger was Dick Holmes.

Waltz died that day, October 25, 1891. They buried him in the Maricopa County Cemetery. The *Phoenix Daily Herald* of October 26, 1891, reported that:

> Jacob Waltz, aged 81 years died at 6 a.m. Sunday, October 25, 1891, and was buried at 10 o'clock this morning, from the residence of Mrs. J.E. Thomas, who had kindly nursed him through his last sickness. Deceased was a native of Germany and spent the last thirty years of his life in Arizona, mining part of the time, ranching and raising chickens. His honest, industrious, amiable character led Mrs. Thomas to care for him during his final days on earth, and he died with a blessing for her on his lips.

The loss of his home and fatal illness added to the mystery of where Old Snowbeard got his gold. Thomas and Reiney said that Waltz wanted them to have the gold under his bed and that he had given them directions to his mine. Holmes said the same thing. It was on the day of Waltz's funeral that the candlestick box turned up empty. Had Waltz wanted to repay Thomas and Reiney for the care they gave him in his last days? Could Waltz have known that if anyone were to find his mine it would have to be a veteran prospector like himself and Dick Holmes? Two distinct views about what Waltz wanted done with his gold and where his secret mine lay hidden. Again, where did Old Snowbeard get his gold? And now, whom to believe—Thomas or Holmes?

3

A GOOD WALTZ

The three people who claimed Old Snowbeard's gold broke off into two teams, Julia Thomas and Reiney Petrasch versus Dick Holmes. One side said Waltz was a kind and generous man. The other side said he was a murderer and a thief. Thomas and Reiney are the ones who claimed a good Waltz.

It was in her shop, with its soda fountain on one side and baked goods on the other, that Thomas met Old Snowbeard. Reiney later told a fellow prospector that, "There was an old German who had forty acres of school land and some chickens, and who had often sold his eggs to the bakery."

Thomas, Reiney and Waltz, became good friends. Because Thomas' husband left her shortly after their arrival in Phoenix, gossip had it that Waltz and Thomas were more than good friends. Rumors said that despite an age difference of over fifty years Thomas became Waltz's mistress. Whatever their relationship, Thomas and Reiney were Waltz's only friends and family in his last years. It is highly likely that Old Snowbeard wanted them to inherit his gold.

According to Thomas, it was shortly after Old Snowbeard bailed her out of debt that he decided to give her and Reiney half of his gold. Thomas told Sims Ely, then editor for the *Arizona Republican* newspaper, that while enjoying a meal at Waltz's place in December of 1890, Waltz told her and Reiney about his mine. According to Ely, Thomas quoted Waltz as saying, "Of course, Julia, you and Reiney couldn't do anything with a mine. You'd have to know about mining for that, and you'd need cash capital. Besides, the mine is in awful rough country, away from water—so rough that you can be right at the mine without seeing it. I wouldn't even try to tell you where the mine is if it wasn't for the cache. But you can't find one without the other. And the cache is different. All you need to do is bring the gold away, and we'll do that when spring comes. I'll give you half of that gold …"

Thomas told Ely that Waltz warned her and Reiney to keep their plan of going to the mine a secret. If certain people knew, they would follow and kill them for the gold. Thomas said Waltz ended the warning by stating he kept the place of his gold mine a secret for a long time. Waltz trusted Thomas and Reiney to do the same.

Since both Thomas and Reiney never learned to read or write, all they had to go by was their skill at remembering exact words spoken. Ely relied on this skill when he recorded what Thomas could remember for his own use. Ely and his partner, Jim Bark, were also searching for the mine. Ely badgered Thomas about Waltz and his gold. Finally, Thomas told Ely that Waltz began to tell her the place of his secret mine, but stopped. Instead, Waltz had decided to take his friends to the mine in the spring when the weather was good for camping. Thomas said they planned to go in March of 1891.

Old Snowbeard never did get the chance to take his friends to his gold mine. The February flood washed his plans away. Thomas said Waltz gave her and Reiney directions to his mine while he was with them the months after the flood. Some say Waltz even made a map for them. When Thomas returned from the funeral and found Waltz's room in shambles, the map had vanished. Thomas claimed someone stole the map and the gold under Waltz's bed the day of the funeral. Reiney said Thomas never went to the funeral. We may never know if Waltz gave Thomas a map or not.

It took Thomas eight months to mourn the loss of Old Snowbeard and build the courage she needed to find the gold. Remembering that Waltz warned her not to go alone Thomas asked Reiney to be her partner. Reiney said he would be willing to go, but only if his older brother Hermann could come too. Reiney sent for Hermann and Thomas began to prepare for the trip. She sold her store to Schooler and Wilson on July 10, 1892, hired a team of horses and bought a wagon. On August 11, 1892, all three headed out to the Superstitions in search for Old Snowbeard's gold.

Just like Old Snowbeard, Thomas made the papers too. The *Arizona Daily Gazette* of August 27, 1892, had the following article.

> A QUEER QUEST
> ANOTHER 'LOST MINE' BEING HUNTED FOR BY A WOMAN.
> Mrs. E. W. Thomas, formerly of the Thomas' ice cream parlors, is now in the Superstition mountains engaged in a work usually deemed strange to woman's sphere. She is prospecting for a lost mine, to the location of which she believes she holds the key. But somehow, she has failed, after two months work to locate the bonanza, though aided by two men. The story of the mine is founded upon the usual death-bed revelations of the ancient miner usual in such cases. There is also a lost cabin connected with it. Its location is supposed to be a short distance back from the western end of the main Superstition mountain.

When the three prospectors made camp in the Superstitions, Thomas was twenty-nine, Hermann was twenty-eight and Reiney was twenty-five years old. Hermann Petrasch was the only one who could write. He later wrote about their trip in a letter to a friend.

> We traveled eastward across the desert from Phoenix, it was extremely hot and hard on the team. The wagon was constantly giving us problems when we crossed the washes. The wagon was soon abandoned some three miles from the face of Superstition Mountain. From this point we walked and used the team to carry our gear. Our plans had included driving the team and wagon as close as possible. We began our search near Weaver's Needle and the west side of Bluff Springs Mountain. The weather was so hot we spent most of the afternoons in the shade and did our searching during the early mornings. Old Jake had left Rhinehart and Julia many clues that placed the mine in the vicinity of Weaver's Needle somewhere on the west side of Bluff Springs Mountain. After three or four weeks of extremely hot weather and the lack of water for the animals we abandoned the search.

The prospectors returned to the Phoenix Township tired, angry and broke. They never searched together again.

After her failure to find Old Snowbeard's gold, Thomas started selling maps showing the exact location of Waltz's mine.

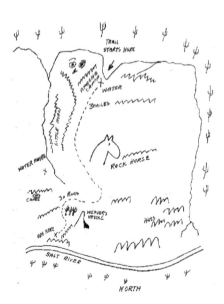

The maps sold for anywhere between $3 to $10 apiece. Back then, $10 meant more than half a month's pay to a cowboy. Perhaps the price depended on which drawing Thomas sold—she had three of them.

Thomas married another prospector by the name of Albert Schaffer. The couple moved to Morristown, Arizona, hoping to strike it rich in gold. Despite her friendship with Waltz, Thomas never did find gold. At the age of fifty-five, Julia Thomas-Schaffer joined her friend Old Snowbeard on December 22, 1917. She died a pauper.

While Thomas had moved on with her life, the Petrasch brothers continued hunting Old Snowbeard's gold. After a fight when Hermann accused Reiney of messing up Waltz's directions, the two brothers parted company. They never spoke to each other again.

Reiney spent the rest of his life hunting Old Snowbeard's gold. The miners of Superior and Globe east of the Superstitions knew all about Reiney's search efforts. Jim Bark, then first president of the Arizona Cattleman's Association, heard about Reiney and tried to help. Bark knew the area and Reiney had the directions. Together, Reiney hoped they could find the mine. As the years passed without any gold, Bark stopped helping and Reiney lost all hope of ever finding Old Snowbeard's gold. On February 4, 1943, Rhinehart Petrasch ended his life with a shotgun.

After fighting with his brother, Hermann Petrasch took a different approach hunting Old Snowbeard's gold. He paid his way by working off and on at the Martin Ranch in the Superstitions. As the years passed, Hermann pasted together wood planks and metal sheets he had scrounged up and called it home. Hermann built his shack on the south bank of Queen Creek next to one of the few sources of year-round water. Close to Hewitt Station on the railroad leading north of Magma, Hermann settled in with the cacti, Ironwood trees and thorny plants. Living the life of a desert hermit, Hermann spent his days scouring the area around Weaver's Needle for Waltz's gold. When Hermann Petrasch died alone and broke in his shack on November 23, 1953, people say he still blamed his brother for forgetting the directions to Old Snowbeard's gold.

Thomas and the Petraschs were not the only ones who could not find Old Snowbeard's gold. They were just among the first. Of course, according to Holmes, they really had no idea where the gold was in the first place.

4

A DYING WALTZ

Richard "Dick" Holmes stayed with Old Snowbeard while Thomas fetched the doctor. Holmes' version of what Waltz said the morning of October 25, 1891, differs from Thomas'. Holmes claimed Waltz gave him the gold under his bed to cover the cost of finding the mine. According to Holmes, Waltz gave him directions because he knew Thomas and Reiney could not find the mine. Only a seasoned prospector like Holmes could get Waltz's gold. Thomas and Reiney said that Holmes stole the gold in the candlestick box. After all, Holmes was already following Waltz, trying to steal the gold mine. We may never know who Old Snowbeard wanted to give his gold to, but we do know that Holmes was alone with Waltz about fifteen minutes as he lay dying.

What happened during those fifteen minutes Holmes was alone with Waltz is still in question today. One group says that Waltz, dying of pneumonia, was too sick to breath, let alone talk. Another group, led by Holmes' son Brownie, claims that Waltz hoped to pass his fortune on to a fellow prospector. Brownie noted all his father told him about Waltz and his gold. Although Brownie's notes will not hold up in a court of law, they do give Holmes' side of the story.

Brownie says his father first heard about Old Snowbeard's gold from a man named John Phipps. Phipps stopped at the ranch where Holmes worked one evening and they shared a bit of biscuits, beans and black walnuts. Later that night, Phipps told Holmes of a mine so rich with pure gold that a man could fill a bathtub with it. The mine was in the big rough mountains south of the Salt River. An old German from Phoenix was working the mine secretly. Phipps told Holmes he had been watching the man for about three years. Holmes asked Phipps why he had not filed a claim on the mine, since the German was not going to. Phipps said he was too afraid of the old German to do such a thing. The next morning, Phipps rode off and Holmes never saw him again.

It was not until 1888 that Holmes met Old Snowbeard in Phoenix. Holmes realized that Waltz was the "German from Phoenix" Phipps talked about. With the help of his friend Gideon Roberts, Holmes took to watching Waltz. The two men hoped Waltz would lead them to his gold mine. Holmes only followed Waltz once into the north end of the Superstitions.

As Brownie noted, his father came around a bend in the trail and "There sitting on a pile of rock, with his rifle in his hands ready for action, and looking the way he had come, sat Jacob Wolz [sic]. There was a ferocious scowl on his face which plainly disclosed the fact that there was murder in his heart."

Holmes quickly made tracks back to town.

Shortly after the clash, Waltz ran across Holmes in Phoenix. According to Brownie, Waltz told his father, "You tried to follow me into the mountains, but don't ever do it again, because the next time, I will surely kill you. I like you Dick, and I don't want to harm you, but remember what I have said."

Dick Holmes decided then and there not to risk following Old Snowbeard into the mountains again.

Waltz's warning did not stop Holmes and Roberts from following Old Snowbeard while he was in Phoenix. Brownie noted that Waltz "always had plenty of money on his person and those of a later day said that he often drank heavily, gambled freely, and boasted of his rich mine in the Superstitions."

Holmes and Roberts hoped that Waltz would get drunk enough to tell the secret hiding place of his gold mine. By the time Waltz was dying in the one-room adobe behind Thomas' shop, Holmes and Roberts were

A DYING WALTZ

watching Waltz in shifts around the clock. So, when Thomas asked Holmes to stay with Old Snowbeard while she fetched the doctor, she did not just ask a stranger. Holmes was waiting for the chance to ask a dying Waltz for directions to his secret gold mine.

According to Brownie, Waltz recognized his father, Holmes, at his bedside and said, "Dick, my time is short and I want to give you the directions to my mine."

As proof of Waltz wanting Holmes to have his gold, Brownie quotes Waltz, including his gasps for air, as saying, "Dick, I know that you wanted to locate this mine ... you tried to follow me once, and I might have killed you. I'm glad that I didn't because I like you ... and there is no one I'd rather see find it, than you."

Holmes told his son that while he sat with Waltz, Old Snowbeard talked about how he found the mine while on his way to Fort McDowell in 1877. Holmes said Waltz came across three Mexicans who had some gold, asked them where they got it and they led him to a hole deep in the Superstitions.

Brownie quotes Waltz as saying, "The hole was only about four feet across and about twelve feet deep. I walked down the ladder and then I got to the bottom. ... There was gold, Dick, wire gold, in the rocks as large as peas. ... Several pounds of ore was lying on the bottom."

Holmes said that the Mexicans were willing to share the mine, but Waltz wanted the gold. Brownie noted Waltz's words as, "I had the gold lust in my blood ... Dick ... I made up my mind to get sole possession of that mine ... at any cost."

Holmes said Waltz shot the Mexicans and that is why he kept the mine a secret, to hide his crime.

Waltz had trouble breathing, which is why Thomas ran for the doctor. Yet, Holmes said Waltz had enough air to confess to more killings during their fifteen minute talk. Brownie notes that Waltz began with the murder of his nephew, who came from Germany to help mine the gold. The nephew wanted to file a claim to work the mine in the open and argued with Waltz about the secret. Holmes told Brownie that Waltz killed his nephew when he got fed up with the fighting.

Brownie quotes Waltz as saying, "I shot him in the forehead between the eyes ... I then took a piece of chain and putting it around his neck ...

dragged him under a shelving rock and where the dirt was soft I dug ... a grave ... and buried him."

In total, Holmes said Waltz confessed to killing seven men to protect his mine. After the last murder, Holmes said Waltz hid the mine so no one could find it. Telling Holmes the hiding spot, Waltz then gave Holmes the gold under his bed to help with the cost of finding his secret mine.

Brownie quotes Waltz as saying, "There's not much there but after I am gone you can have it. ... It's in a box under my bed ... take it ... I know there is enough to grubstake you for a while anyway, Dick."

Brownie says that his father asked Waltz if he dug up all the gold.

Brownie tells people that Waltz answered with, "There is enough gold to make twenty men millionaires."

Holmes told his son that those were some of the last words Waltz uttered. Waltz closed his eyes, took a deep breath and died. Holmes said that a few minutes later Reiney showed up.

Reiney agreed that Holmes was alone with a dying Waltz for about fifteen minutes. Reiney also said that Old Snowbeard died before he could get there. Reiney was one of the first to doubt that Waltz had such a long talk with Holmes—Waltz was too sick to talk. Thomas and Reiney later said Holmes lied and stole the gold from under Waltz's bed. We may never know who told the truth, but we do know that Holmes had some of Old Snowbeard's gold. Brownie always said it was his father that took the ore from the candlestick box.

Records show that early in 1892, Holmes sold some of Old Snowbeard's gold. Holmes and Gideon Roberts bought supplies with the money and made their first trip into the Superstitions. They did not find Waltz's mine. A few weeks later Gideon Roberts died.

Holmes searched alone for Old Snowbeard's gold until his son Brownie joined him in 1908 at the age of sixteen. After his father's death, Brownie continued searching hoping to prove his father told the truth. In his notes, Brownie said that people believed Thomas, instead of his father.

"At last," Brownie wrote, "when all her stories were proven without foundation, she admitted that my father was the sole possessor of the secret of the Lost Dutchman of the Superstitions."

Brownie sold the rest of Old Snowbeard's gold ore to pay medical bills. The person who bought the ore had a pair of cufflinks and cigarette lighter made from the gold.

He also gave some of it to the University of Arizona, School of Mines, so experts could figure out where it originated. Raw ore's matrix, the stuff besides gold, works like a fingerprint telling where it comes from. When the experts said the ore came from an unknown source, they agreed that Waltz's gold did not stem from any of the known mines in Arizona. The experts' findings also show that an untapped source of gold may still be in the desert outside Apache Junction.

Julia Thomas, Rhinehart and Hermann Petrasch, Gideon Roberts, Dick and Brownie Holmes all claimed they had the secret to Waltz's gold, but none of them found it. Old Snowbeard's gold soon became a nationwide mystery. The invention of the printing press in the late nineteenth century gave birth to a new source of information, the newspaper. Reporters anxious for a good story about the Wild West and lost gold mines only added to the ever-growing mystery. Where did Old Snowbeard get his gold?

5

NEWSPAPERS AND LEGENDS

Shortly after the end of the Civil War, a new breed of story-tellers joined in the yarns about Old Snowbeard's gold. Two of these men, Joseph Pulitzer and William Randolph Hearst, then owners of the two largest American newspapers, started a new war—the fight for newspaper sales. Pulitzer won a major battle when he published the first comic strip in his newspaper the *New York Sunday World* in 1895. When Hearst hired the artist and printed the first colored comics in 1896, he won a battle for his paper the *New York Journal*. Soon both men turned to printing stories about the Wild West and lost gold mines.

As the battle increased, reporters wrote more and more about Waltz's lost gold. The wilder the story the better, even if it was true or not. One of the local newsmen, Sims Ely, together with his friend and ranch owner, Jim Bark, hunted Old Snowbeard's gold. As word got out, treasure hunters passed through Bark's ranch, each with their own idea as to the mine's hiding place. It was Jim Bark who dubbed it the "Lost Dutchman Gold Mine." From then on, Old Snowbeard became known as the Dutchman, because his birthplace was *Deutschland*.

Some of the first news printed about the Lost Dutchman Gold Mine appeared in the Phoenix paper, *The Saturday Review*. On November 17, 1894, the headline read:

> A MYTHICAL MINE
> STORY OF A LOST CLAIM IN THE SUPERSTITION MOUNTAINS, 'DUTCH JACOB'S' SECRET
> PHOENIX PEOPLE NOW HUNTING FOR THE TREASURE WITH PROSPECTS OF SUCCESS.

August 25, 1895, another headline read:

> DUTCH JACOB'S MINE
> HIDDEN WEALTH ONCE KNOWN IN THE SUPERSTITIONS.
> A WELL KNOWN MINER WISHES TO FIND IT.

Besides printing news about the searches for the mine, new reports came out about how Waltz got his gold. Needing to defend their scoop, reporters turned to telling why Old Snowbeard kept his mine a secret. The article printed in 1895 gives hints of this trend. The last lines were, "The Dutch Jacob Mine is a reality, and although it may not be found it is highly probable it will be. One thing certain, the old man took great precaution to conceal the property which must be very rich as he got gold almost single handed."

The news of the Lost Dutchman Gold Mine spread throughout the country. Reports of Waltz finding the Apaches' Thundergod gold, or Waltz coming across a lost Mexican mine hit the newsstands. Printed so often the news became accepted as fact. With the help of the printing press, the legend of the Lost Dutchman Gold Mine flourished.

The report about Old Snowbeard finding the Thundergod's gold starts with an Army surgeon named Abram Thorne. Depending on who reported the story, Thorne either saved the life of an Apache Chief's son or cured all the tribe's children of an eye disease. Either way, in a show of thanks, Apache braves blindfolded Thorne one night and led him to the sacred place of their Thundergod's gold.

As the story goes, Thorne had to wear a blindfold to protect the Thundergod's secret treasure. Native American lore has it that the Thundergod used the Superstitions as a hiding place for his vast treasure of gold. The Thundergod turned anyone daring to steal his gold into stone. One tale says that the stone pillars on the north end of the Superstitions are thieves caught by the Thundergod. The Thundergod told the Apaches to let Thorne take some of his gold as a gift, but only once. Thorne tried later on to find the place where in a canyon with high walls yellow metal glistened in the sunlight, but he failed.

The Thundergod is really Pima lore, but Apaches were making headlines on the East Coast and reporters gave Geronimo's people the credit. The reporters also said Thorne was the first white man to see Old Snowbeard's gold in the fall of 1865—or so legend has it.

The other common tale of how Old Snowbeard got his gold involves Mexican miners killed by Apaches. The story started in 1901. A Prescott, Arizona, newspaper printed the first report of Waltz finding the remains of the *El Sombrero* mine. The Sombrero mine got its name from a nearby peak that looked like a hat. The news said the peak was Weaver's Needle and the mine was one of eight owned by a family named Peralta. The Peraltas came from Sonora, Mexico to mine gold from *El Sombrero* for many years.

The Mexican miners story tells of one last fatal trip made by the Peraltas to clear out the Sombrero mine before it became the property of the United States in 1848. On their way back through the Superstitions, Apaches attacked the party of over 400 men and mules carrying saddlebags full of gold. Only one Mexican survived the attack, Manual Peralta. He was the 12-year-old heir of Don Miguel Peralta. The story ends with Waltz finding *El Sombrero*; the mine once worked by the Peralta family.

The story printed in 1901, was only the first tale of Waltz finding a lost Peralta gold mine. Because Arizona once belonged to Mexico, people readily believed the news. In addition, the name Peralta is very common down around Sonora, Mexico. Anyone could come across a Peralta or Peralto south of the Mexican-American border. The story about Waltz finding a lost Peralta gold mine is so full of half-truths that it is hard to verify. Perhaps that is why it spread so fast.

Other news appeared linking Waltz's gold with the Peralta's mine. Some said that Waltz saved Manual Peralta, the only survivor of the Apache attack, from a card game fight while in Sonora, Mexico. To show thanks, Peralta gave Waltz a map to his family mine in the Superstitions. Peralta told Waltz the gold was a gift. Others reported that Peralta hired Waltz to find *El Sombrero* in exchange for half the gold. This story ends with Waltz killing the last of the Peraltas and stealing the gold. All the news forever linked Old Snowbeard with the Peraltas—or so legend has it.

After the tale of Peralta gold, reporters began writing about Waltz having a partner, Jacob Weiser. A popular legend grew in the printed words, one that made Waltz out to be a killer. Stories said the Waltz killed his partner, claiming Apaches attacked them while they were working at the mine. Other reports said that Apaches attacked Weiser, but Waltz left him for dead and ran off to Tucson. Then the news said Weiser survived, made his way to a Pima village and died under the care of a doctor named Walker. By the 1920s, word spread that Old Snowbeard killed his partner, Jacob Weiser—or so legend has it.

Some of the tales printed about how Waltz got his gold were far from the truth, but they helped sell tons of newspapers. Since the Arizona Rangers were busy rounding up outlaws at the time, one story makes Waltz out to be one. They say that Waltz stole high-grade ore while working at the Vulture Mine outside Wickenburg. Waltz then hid the ore in a cave in the Superstitions and talked about a mine to fool the law. When proven that Waltz never worked at the Vulture Mine, the story changed to Waltz acting as a go-between for other highgraders. Waltz received a portion of the loot as pay and hid it in the Superstitions. Another report said Waltz got his gold by robbing mule-trains, stagecoaches and anyone else crossing the Superstitions.

Newspaper reports and word of mouth grew into bizarre tales. Some say Waltz found a cache of Spanish gold left by Jesuit priests. Others say that when the stars were right, Waltz followed a moonbeam shining through the eye of Weaver's Needle. At the end of the beam was the mine. One story

NEWSPAPERS AND LEGENDS

has it that Waltz's partner gave the doctor who took care of him a map to the Lost Dutchman. Reports had it that the Peraltas made sandstone maps to *El Sombrero* and the Dutchman mine. Still more reports said that Waltz gave Dick Holmes a map showing a Palo Verde tree with an arm pointing toward the gold. Perhaps this report led a Pawtucket, Rhode Island man to send a letter to the Phoenix Chamber of Commerce in 1934. The letter told readers how to locate Old Snowbeard's gold. "Find the gigantic sahuaro [sic] cactus, twisted like a creature in a nightmare, and there will be the fabulously rich Lost Dutchman Gold Mine."

All the news about Old Snowbeard and his mysterious gold helped create the Lost Dutchman Gold Mine legend. As reports spread, treasure seekers flooded the Superstitions. Some had newspapers giving clues left by Waltz. Others had books fresh off the shelf telling where to find Old Snowbeard's gold. Some even had a map, showing the exact spot of the Lost Dutchman mine. The people rushing to hunt Old Snowbeard's mine made his gold even more mysterious.

6

DUTCHMAN HUNTERS ABOUND

By the end of the 1920s, legends about the Lost Dutchman Gold Mine were firmly in print. Greenhorns and prospectors flocked to the Superstitions hunting Old Snowbeard's gold. Some made discoveries. Some made claims. A few stayed and some lost their lives. The 1930s and 1940s became a time for Dutchman Hunters to abound in the Superstition Wilderness of Arizona.

One of the greenhorns that rushed to the Superstitions in the 1930s had a map he believed would lead him to the Peralta's Sombrero Mine. Adolph Ruth got his map from his son Erwin, who got it from a man in Mexico, who said he got it from his mother's side of the family, the Peraltas.

Ruth really had two maps. One showed a Peralta mine in California. While searching for this mine in 1919, Ruth fell from a ledge and broke his hip. Doctors used a silver plate to mend the bone. From then on, Ruth had a limp and used a cane.

After the accident, Ruth returned to his government job in Washington, DC. His son hoped he had given up on finding lost gold mines. For eleven years, it seemed that Ruth forgot the maps his son gave him. Then, in the spring of 1931, Ruth retired from his job and asked his son to help him find the Peralta mine in Arizona.

Erwin Ruth refused to go with his dad hoping he could change his father's mind. Erwin knew his dad could not make the trip on his own. But against his son's wishes, Ruth packed his bags and left with a friend in the family car on May 4, 1931. By the time they reached Arizona, Ruth's friend took one look at the desolate desert and hitched a ride back home. Eager to find Old Snowbeard's gold, Ruth went on by himself, driving to the Barkley Ranch in the Superstition wilderness.

Ruth hounded workers at the Barkley Ranch. He asked everyone to point out landmarks on his map and water holes in the mountains. Tex Barkley, the ranch owner, told Ruth not to go into the Superstitions alone. Barkley even said he would escort Ruth, but Ruth would have to wait until Barkley shipped his cattle to market. Ruth waited a whole month, but no longer. He swayed two ranch hands to pack him in on horseback and help setup camp at Willow Spring. The two men settled Ruth about a mile west of Weaver's Needle and returned to the ranch. Alone, Ruth ignored Barkley's advice—do not hunt the Lost Dutchman by yourself!

Barkley's warning had not been given lightly. In summer, desert temperatures can reach well over 110 degrees. The blazing hot sun can cook a steak in a black skillet without a fire. Authorities warn people to have plenty of water and to watch the elderly, the very young and even their pets for signs of heatstroke. Poisonous rattlesnakes, scorpions, tarantulas and centipedes thrive in the Superstitions. The spiny desert plants and cacti can cause serious infections that, if left to fester can kill an adult. There is even one variety of cacti nicknamed the Jumping Cactus. A slight brush of this cactus and hundreds of fine needles jump onto the person who did the brushing. In addition, one wrong step in the loose shale, sandy washes or uneven mountain sides can easily mean a twisted ankle or a broken hip.

Ruth went into the Superstitions at the age of sixty-two. He walked with a limp and used a cane. Ruth started searching for the Lost Dutchman on June 13, 1931, during the hottest time of the year in the desert wilderness.

When Barkley returned from his cattle roundup several days later, he heard that Ruth went into the wilderness on his own. Barkley quickly got on his horse and rode out to the Willow Spring campsite. He wanted to check on Ruth. The camp was empty.

DUTCHMAN HUNTERS ABOUND

Barkley spent several hours searching the immediate area, but found no signs of Ruth. Getting on his horse, Barkley rushed back to his ranch. He had to call the Pinal and Maricopa County Sheriff Departments to report Ruth missing. Since the area Ruth planned to search includes both counties, the boundary line runs right through, Barkley knew a rescue would involve both departments.

On June 18, 1931, a posse started searching for Ruth. Rescuers scoured the area around Weaver's Needle for days. Erwin Ruth joined in and hired a plane, thinking that taking pictures from the air might help find his father. But still, no signs of Ruth.

Newspapers all over the world reported that Ruth vanished. For forty-five days, the posse hunted on horseback and combed the area on foot. Finally, the Sheriff departments presumed Ruth dead and gave up searching. Then on December 13, 1931, the *Arizona Republic* front page headline read:

> SKULL BELIEVED THAT OF MISSING PROSPECTOR FOUND IN MOUNTAINS.

The Phoenix newspaper sponsored a group to explore ancient ruins in the Superstitions with Brownie Holmes as their guide. When Brownie held the skull up for a picture, he noticed two holes, one on each temple. The holes led Brownie and others to believe that someone shot Ruth.

A few days later Tex Barkley and a Deputy Sheriff found Ruth's headless skeleton in West Boulder Canyon. They knew it belonged to Ruth because of the silver plate within the scattered bones. In Ruth's coat were some papers, a letter to his wife and children, a hand-drawn map and the bottom half of a note. The letter described how he set up camp the first two days and ended with "I'll gradually put things ship-shape. Sometime tomorrow morning I'll prospect some. I left my car at the Barkley Ranch. Love, A. Ruth."

The torn note read:

> It lies within an imaginary circle whose diameter is not more than five miles and whose center is marked by the Weaver Needle, about 2,500 ft. high—among a confusion of lesser peaks and mountain masses of basaltic rock. ...

On the bottom Ruth wrote the words "*Veni, Vidi, Vici.*"—I came, I saw, I conquered.

On record, Ruth died from natural causes, either lack of water or need for food. Off record, it was murder. Some say the two ranch hands shot Ruth, stole his map, took his car, picked up their girlfriends and drove to Phoenix. Others believe that because Ruth talked so freely about his map, someone followed him and when he found the mine, shot him with a high-powered rifle. The killer then chopped off Ruth's head dragging it and the body to separate canyons to hide the crime. Taking Ruth's map, the killer then left the area to wait until things cooled down.

Arizona authorities said the holes in Ruth's skull could have come from the horn of a Javelina pig. Erwin Ruth and his brother could not believe what they heard. They sent their father's skull to a family friend who worked as a research scientist at the Smithsonian Institution. The scientist said the holes came from a gunshot wound, most likely a high-powered rifle. Later on, the scientist said that someone used a .44 or .45 caliber, old model Army revolver to kill Ruth.

Believing their father murdered the Ruth brothers asked Senator Carl Hayden for help. They told the Senator how Arizona authorities refused to find their father's killer because he died of natural causes. They asked the Senator to demand a formal inquest to prove the true cause of death, murder. Maricopa County Sheriff J.D. Adams told the Senator that since there was no evidence of foul play, it would be a waste of time and money to hold an inquest. To this day, Ruth's death certificate says he died of natural causes.

Because of Adolph Ruth, Old Snowbeard's gold became a worldwide mystery. Newspapers all over the world reported Ruth's mysterious death. Ruth's tragic end should have stopped the flood of prospectors rushing to the Superstitions. Instead, the news brought even more Dutchman Hunters to Arizona during the 1930s.

One of the hunters, Thomas Wiggins, thought he found Old Snowbeard's gold in 1932. Wiggins ran into Superior southeast of the Superstitions with his fists tightly wrapped around marble-size nuggets of gold. The gold sold for almost $50 an ounce, a very rich find. President Roosevelt set gold prices at $35 an ounce in 1934. Since Old Snowbeard had equally rich ore, treasure seekers rushed to the area believing Wiggins found the Lost Dutchman. By the end of the day, Wiggins had to hire armed guards to watch his claim.

The gold rush Wiggins created lasted only a couple of days. As Wiggins dug deeper into the earth, the gold became less and less. Wiggins had found a fluke, a small deposit of gold. Old Snowbeard had a vein of gold. Some said a vein wider than a foot and deeper than a mile. When Wiggins' diggings had no gold, treasure hunters left as quickly as they came. The Dutchman's gold was still out there, somewhere in the Superstitions.

A 1932 *Oakland Tribune* article about Adolph Ruth launched Walter Gassler on his Dutchman hunting career. Gassler spent two years reading up on the lost mine until 1934 when the Arizona Biltmore Hotel offered him a job as a pastry chef in Phoenix. Although he did not become a chef, Gassler stayed in Arizona. He moved to what would later become Apache Junction, pitching a tent next to an empty drug store. In 1934, Apache Junction had four cabins for houses, one restaurant for food and a lonely gas station for fuel.

After setting up his tent, Gassler found the local Dutchman expert, Tex Barkley. They became fast friends and Gassler spent many hours in Barkley's ranch house library talking about Old Snowbeard's mysterious gold. Gassler kept a diary, making notes on what he read and talks he had. Surprised by all the different stories he learned about Waltz and his gold, Gassler came up with his own idea. Gassler decided Waltz found the Sombrero mine that once belonged to the Peraltas from Mexico.

Running his idea by Barkley one night, Gassler asked about Adolph Ruth's death. Barkley said someone killed Ruth for his map. Gassler noted what Barkley said in his diary:

> Tex found the body, got a mule and Tom Dickens, a cow puncher; they put his body in burlap and transported it to Black Top Mesa hoping it would be found there. Again, I asked him why. He explained that a few years ago somebody claimed they found the Lost Dutchman and about 200 people came stampeding back there and scattered his "Cattle to Kingdom come—clear up to four peaks." It took about 60 days and extra cowhands to recover all the cattle and he said, "not ever again."

Gassler also decided that night that despite his moving Ruth's body, Barkley was a good man who could help him find the Lost Dutchman.

In his hunt for Waltz's mine, Gassler bagged some quartz with traces of gold. When he stumbled onto an area with charcoal pits and grinding stones scattered about, Gassler felt he located the Peralta's main mining camp. Soon Gassler found what he believed to be Old Snowbeard's secret gold mine. He later recorded the event in his diary:

> My heart jumped out of my mouth; hell, I was at the Lost Dutchman. But, the task proved too much in the end. I had to give it up. Oh, I dug all right but to no end. There was one hole already there and I thought Tex, maybe, had already tried it.
>
> You must remember I could only prospect in summer. I had to work in wintertime. No water up there and it was two miles to Charleybois Spring and a long way to the watering hole in Peter's Canyon.

Gassler worked as long as he could at uncovering the mine, but he ran out of time and money. "Then came the time when I told Tex, I just could not keep up," Gassler wrote, "either I would have to give up prospecting or my family."

Gassler gave up prospecting and returned to his family.

By the 1940s, there were so many Dutchman Hunters in the Superstitions that people started using nicknames to tell them apart. They called Barry Storm, who filed two claims in the area, the "Hans Christian Anderson of the Superstitions."

Storm got the name after he wrote two nonfiction books about Old Snowbeard and his gold. The books should have sold as fiction novels. One of Storm's books became the 1949 movie *Lust for Gold*, starring Glenn Ford as the Dutchman. After seeing the film, another Dutchman Hunter said the movie "is a deliciously awful motion picture based loosely—ever so loosely—on the Lost Dutchman legend."

In a way, Storm's nickname is a compliment; Hans Christian Anderson is famous for outstanding fairy tales.

Storm's wild tales made the "Resident Philosopher" so angry that he wrote a book to tell Waltz's real story. Ludwig Rosecrans got his nickname because he loved to discuss the meaning of life with anyone who would listen. He came to the Superstitions in April 1946. After finding gold lying on the surface of a sunbaked clearing near Weaver's Needle, Rosecrans thought he found the Lost Dutchman. He quickly moved into the Superstitions and built a small cabin where he could see the top of Weaver's Needle.

Visitors enjoyed talking with Rosecrans at his cabin in the Superstitions. He had a good philosophy toward life and openly shared his views about the Lost Dutchman. One of Rosecrans' two and a half claims rewarded him with sixteen tons of gold ore once in 1952. The ore turned out to have about half an ounce of gold per ton, barely enough to cover the cost of digging it up. Rosecrans took the bad news well. He told people, "I came out here to get rich, but I got educated instead."

When the Resident Philosopher, Ludwig Rosecrans, died on April 7, 1986, Dutchman Hunters and friends all felt the loss of a good man.

Another of the favored Dutchman Hunters arriving in the Superstitions during the 1940s was Albert Erland Morrow. Dubbed the "Samaritan of Superstition Mountain," Morrow welcomed visitors to his peaceful camp. He made a six-by-eight foot tent his home in Needle Canyon. The tall, skinny man, usually wearing khakis and a baseball cap, offered a hot cup of coffee and friendly conversation about the Lost Dutchman.

Morrow believed that Old Snowbeard found the Peralta's Sombrero mine. He also believed deeply in God. During his twenty-one years in the Superstitions, the Samaritan copied the Bible by hand three times.

Morrow proved he had the correct nickname when he willingly helped anyone in need by providing food and shelter. Sheriff Deputies and Forest Rangers usually went to Morrow's camp first when hunting lost travelers. Often, Morrow gave the vital clue that led rescue workers to lost or wounded hikers. He kept a close eye on visitors to the Superstitions and knew where they planned to wander in the harsh terrain.

Although Morrow never found Old Snowbeard's gold, he did find what he called the Waltz Rock. The rock, with the date 1878 and the initials J.W. carved in it, led Morrow to believe he set his tent in the same spot Old Snowbeard camped. He said he could not find the Dutchman mine because an earthquake in 1887 buried it.

The Samaritan of Superstition Mountain who helped so many died a lonely death. A young friend, invited to spend a few days with Morrow, arrived to find the camp empty. After searching the area for three days, the Sheriff's posse returned to Morrow's camp deciding to search again in a nearby tunnel. One of the Deputies noticed a stench coming from under a huge boulder above and went to find the cause—he found Morrow's body. The posse felt that since the tunnel probably flooded during the heavy rains the previous weekend Morrow escaped and sat under a leaning boulder to dry off. Morrow's plan was solid, but the boulder was not. The rains washed enough dirt away to dislodge the slab, which came crashing down to kill Morrow instantly. Morrow once said, "If I die here, it is the will of God and the 'Old Dutchman' has won another round."

Other Dutchman Hunters died in the Superstitions during the 1930s and 1940s. Like Ruth, some skeletons had no head. Others died from gunshots. Perhaps the legend on the Dutchman Monument, dedicated in 1938, better describes the time.

DUTCHMAN HUNTERS ABOUND

> Here lie the remains of Snowbeard, the Dutchman, who in this mountain shot three men to steal a rich gold mine from Spanish pioneers, killed eight more to hold its treasure, then died in 1892 without revealing its location. Dozens of searchers have met mysterious death in the canyons there, yet the ore lies unrevealed. Indians say this is the curse of the thunder gods on white men in whom the craving for gold is strong. Beware lest you too succumb to the lure of the Lost Dutchman Mine in Superstition Mountain.

Whoever wrote the words might have made a mistake about the year Old Snowbeard died, but the message is clear. Hunting the Lost Dutchman could become a life-threatening career.

7

FEUDING ON THE NEEDLE

> The second conflict began in 1956 but did not become serious until early Oct. 1959 when Justice of the Peace Norman L. Teason acting as a one man grand jury in his court room at Apache Junction ordered Edgar E. Piper, and Celeste Maria Jones to bring their squabbling to an end. ... Teason further ordered all parties involved to surrender their high-powered rifles to the Sheriff.

So reported the *Apache Sentinel* on New Year's Day following the year Barbie® met America and the television show *Bonanza* first aired. The two feuding parties, Celeste Maria Jones and Edgar "Ed" Piper, were two Dutchman Hunters camped within shooting distance of each other at the base of Weaver's Needle. Jones and Piper appeared in front of Justice Teason because Jones started using her favorite .30-06 rifle to take potshots at Piper and his men. To get even, Piper crept into Jones' camp one night and stole her bullets. Both complained to the law, who took their rifles away.

Justice Teason thought that without long-range weapons the two adults bullying each other over mining claims and waterholes would quit the shooting.

Jones, an odd woman with a heavy dose of gold fever, came to the Superstitions in 1949. She filed the first of three claims near Weaver's Needle on December 2. An African-American woman from California, Jones said she and Julia Thomas came from the same family. People gossiped about Jones, just as they had about Old Snowbeard. Many wondered how she got the money to pay for her hunting trips into the Superstitions. Some say she was a famous opera singer with plenty of rich adoring fans to finance her ventures. Others say she sold mining shares to fellow church members for a dollar apiece. She did have money and caused quite a stir in Apache Junction and Phoenix. Jones would appear in town wearing tight-fitting gold pants, sunglasses, a wide brimmed hat and tennis shoes.

Jones also confused visitors to her camp. She would welcome them warmly with a friendly smile, yet the pistol on her hip, rifle in hand and armed guards at her side caused many to wonder if they were safe. Robert Sikorsky, a young geologist hired by Jones as the gold expert, described the camp as "one of the most bizarre groups ever to set foot in the Superstitions."

FEUDING ON THE NEEDLE

The bizarre group, camped in East Boulder Canyon just south of Weaver's Needle, led Sikorsky to write a book about the time he spent hunting Old Snowbeard's gold with Jones.

When Sikorsky worked for Jones, she had two other hired hands as well. Raymond, a Mexican who drove a powder blue 1952 Chevy, made supply runs and provided rides to and from Phoenix. Louie, a small man with a big mustache, was the camp's mountaineer. Sikorsky said that Louie "could move across the terrain like a water bug across a pool of water."

Quite a few people thought Jones to be crazy. Her visits to an old Spanish gypsy to receive blessing and good fortune helped fuel the idea. She also thought that Weaver's Needle was hollow and that little people living in it guarded the gold.

"Nothing would produce a stranger feeling than to sit in the Jones camp," Sikorsky said in his book, "and suddenly hear Maria's voice break out in a strange chant. ...When she sang nothing made sense—it was a mumbo-jumbo foreign to both me and the others in the camp. Perhaps it was something she made up, perhaps something the gypsy had taught her. ...Maria would say she was singing to the people in the Needle, the keepers of the treasure."

Jones' methods of prospecting were also bizarre. She had her men drill tunnels straight through the sides of the Needle. They used ropes to build ladders to the top of the Needle. Jones even ordered her men to use all her dynamite to blow up the Needle. Sikorsky started thinking about quitting after that.

Sikorsky's first day up on the rope ladder showed signs of how Jones felt about guns. He heard shooting down below. Thinking Jones and Louie were in trouble Sikorsky rushed down Weaver's Needle. He heard laughter as he got closer to camp. Realizing that his friends were not in danger, Sikorsky asked about the shooting. In reply, Sikorsky quotes Jones as saying, "I saw a Gila monster right there in those rocks and emptied my pistol at him."

When Louie looked up and shrugged his shoulders, Sikorsky knew Jones often emptied her pistol. Soon, Jones had something besides Gila monsters to shoot at.

In 1952, a tall, skinny man moved from Idaho to Arizona. He had no family and showed no signs of being rich. The 62-year-old man, Ed Piper, knew that Spanish priests left a huge pile of gold in a cave somewhere on Weaver's Needle.

Piper filed five mining claims near the natural monument named after Pauline Weaver, one of Arizona's first fur trappers. On February 9, 1956, when Piper filed his first mining claim he named it after the then popular movie, *The Thing*. By the time he appeared in front of Justice Teason in 1959, Piper listed his address as Weaver's Needle, Superstition Mountains, Arizona. And that was part of the problem; Jones did not want a neighbor.

Although Jones had a place in Phoenix, she considered Weaver's Needle her vacation home and the waterhole in East Boulder Canyon as her kitchen sink. Jones must have thought Piper very rude when in 1952 he built a shelter and planted fruit trees in her living room. Jones demanded that Piper leave the area—she was there first. The quick tempered Piper with a .357 magnum strapped firmly to his hip told Jones she was crazy. Piper planned to stay until he found Old Snowbeard's gold.

Sikorsky writes about the growing feud between Piper and Jones in his book. He said the two started out by arguing over who was on whose land. "While I was with her, the squabble over who could walk this trail and who could climb that hill began to come to a head," Sikorsky wrote. "There was no love lost between the two and they did their best to avoid seeing each other."

Sikorsky went against Jones' wishes and called on her neighbor a couple of times. Sikorsky always visited Piper unarmed to prove he was not an enemy. On his visits, Piper would ask questions about Jones and instruct Sikorsky to tell her to stay off his claims and away from his waterhole. Piper hated having Jones on his property. Sikorsky quotes Piper as saying, "There is plenty of room elsewhere for her to do her prospecting."

When Piper dug a well, Jones took to what she called "dusting their dirty pants." She started shooting into Piper's camp, close enough to the men to kick dirt up onto their pants. But it was only when Piper returned from a supply trip to find his cabin in ruins, his fruit trees lying on the ground, and the water in his well spoiled that he started shooting back.

One day in early April 1959, as Sikorsky dozed in his tent after eating a large meal he heard a thud on the ground just outside. A few seconds later he heard the crack from a rifle. "The thud and the rifle echo came again," Sikorsky said, "and I realized someone was shooting into our camp."

Sikorsky, Jones and Louie dove behind the dynamite boxes. They stayed for hours, waiting for the cover of night before creeping back to their tents. Sikorsky quit the next morning.

The Samaritan of Superstition Mountain, Al Morrow, tried several times to stop the feuding. When either Piper or Jones came by for a visit, Morrow tried to make peace by asking them to lay down their arms. They told Morrow to mind his own business. Even after losing their rifles to Justice Teason, the two continued their shooting, only at closer range. Piper and Jones still had their pistols.

The Piper-Jones feud became the talk of Apache Junction. As a joke, a Bar Owner posted two signs in his place. One read, "Enlist in Piper's Army here." The other read, "Enlist in Celeste Jones's Army here." Several heavily armed men must have taken the signs seriously, for the first war casualty soon followed.

Piper swore that on November 11, 1959, while he and his friend Robert Crandall were on their way up to a digging site on Weaver's Needle, a man named Robert St. Marie stepped out from behind a boulder. Piper told the Sheriff that he asked St. Marie what he was doing there, if he needed any help. In answer and according to Piper, St. Marie pulled out his revolver and said, "I will talk with this."

Crandall told the Sheriff that St. Marie was under orders from Jones to shoot them if they dared to place foot on Weaver's Needle. For whatever reason, St. Marie approached the men with his gun drawn. Piper quickly drew his .357 magnum from its holster. As he dove for cover, Piper fired three times as fast as he could pull the trigger. St. Marie died and Piper went before the Judge.

The Judge set Piper free, ruling the killing as an act of self-defense. Then, fourteen days later, Ralph Thomas, a friend of Jones, shot and killed Lavern Rowlee in self-defense too.

Although Rowlee's death stopped the gunplay, the Piper-Jones feud never truly ended until Piper became sick and left the area on June 24, 1962. With no one to fight, Jones hired Vance Bacon to replace Sikorsky and became even crazier in her prospecting. Bacon died on March 26, 1963, when he fell from a rope dangling on the side of Weaver's Needle. The Forest Rangers tried to get Jones to take the ropes down and allow free access to the area. Rumor has it that shortly after Bacon died Jones went insane and told her men to blow up the Needle. Instead, the men left their crazy boss, leaving Jones to wander off and die alone. Others say that Piper's death drove Jones over the edge and she ended up in the Arizona State Hospital for the Insane.

From 1959 to 1963, while Jones and Piper were feuding on the Needle, other Dutchman Hunters took their chances on finding Old Snowbeard's gold and died. The headless skeleton of Franz Harrier, an Australian exchange student, showed up in the area on October 23, 1960. The body of Walter J. Mowry from Denver, Colorado, surprised a hiker on March 21, 1961. Later that year, the body of another victim appeared. Charles Bohen, from Salt Lake City, Utah, died from a bullet through the heart. In a drastic move to stop Dutchman Hunters traveling to the Superstitions and their death, the Pinal County Sheriff issued the following warning sometime around 1963.

> Too many foolish people are going into Superstition Mountain, hoping to find the Lost Dutchman Gold Mine. That's a wild and rugged range. There are many deep canyons, high cliffs, dangerous slides. It is very easy to get lost. Since there is little water, and game is hard to get, you can quickly die of thirst or starve. There is also danger from fanatics who shoot at people; several persons have been mysteriously killed.
>
> Unless you have experience guides and are fully equipped and armed, my advice to all citizens is to STAY AWAY FROM UP THERE.

8

MODERN HUNTERS

During the early sixties, the Pinal County Sheriff was not the only one to worry about "fanatics who shoot at people." The rest of America faced the same problem. Gunshots ended the lives of President Kennedy and Martin Luther King, Jr. By the mid-sixties, with Piper and Jones gone, things began to settle down in the Superstitions. America started discovering the mystery of space and Old Snowbeard's gold began luring more modern day hunters. One of these hunters, Glenn Magill, had a private detective business in Oklahoma City. Magill had never heard of the lost gold until an attorney from Denver, Colorado, told him about it. The attorney believed that by "using modern methods—particularly a helicopter," he and Magill would be the ones to find Old Snowbeard's gold.

The attorney chose Magill as a partner because of his award-winning private detective work. Applying the same skill that won him the award, Magill started a different type of missing person case in 1964. He set out to find the Lost Dutchman Gold Mine.

Magill began his case by reading through all the information the attorney had on the Dutchman. Then Magill flew to Phoenix to look up public records and talk with people who knew Waltz personally. Magill found out that Waltz cashed in a fortune of gold ore, spent very little of it and hid the rest in the Superstition Mountains of Arizona.

After sorting through all the stories about the Lost Dutchman Gold Mine, separating fact from fiction, Magill hired a helicopter to fly over the Superstitions in December 1964. For the first time in the history of Dutchman Hunters, Magill used aerial photography as a modern method of prospecting. He took pictures using a camera for still photographs and a movie camera for 8-millimeter film. This way, Magill could study the area from the comfort of his home in Oklahoma.

By using modern technology along with his highly tuned detective skills, Magill created a solid missing gold case. He gathered enough information to conclude that the Lost Dutchman and the Peralta Sombrero Mine were the same thing. Excited, Magill called Denver to let the attorney know of his guess work and find out how he would get paid. But it turned out that the attorney had died, leaving Magill to hunt Old Snowbeard's gold on his own.

It was not until March of 1965 that Magill made his next trip into the Superstitions. This time he hiked in on foot and brought a friend. Magill knew he had to have a partner—too many single prospectors before him died. On this trip, Magill set out to confirm leads he came up with during his initial work. Finding charcoal beds left by Spanish miners made Magill feel close to the Peralta gold mine. On another trip that fall, Magill went back to the north end of Bluff Spring Mountain and dug up a Spanish mule-shoe. Next to the shoe, Magill found some gold-speckled quartz. The discovery of gold ended Magill's logical detective work—he now had a heavy dose of gold fever.

When he returned to Oklahoma, Magill contacted Erwin Ruth to see if he had any copies of his father's map. To his surprise, Magill received traced copies of three maps once belonging to Adolph Ruth. The maps gave clues leading to the Peralta's *El Sombrero* mine in Arizona. Magill studied the maps for months, trying to figure out the clues. In mid-April, with the help of his Spanish speaking wife, Magill had his answers and decided to make another trip. With the maps and the help of some trusted partners, Magill knew he could find the Lost Dutchman Gold Mine.

Magill came up with some rules that anyone joining his gold-safari had to agree with. The rules were that everyone would equally share all expenses and all gold, but Magill would get the first $5,000 as pay for his detective work. Magill would also be the group's spokesperson, which meant that only he could write their story and talk to the press. Six men agreed to Magill's terms.

After signing the Dutchman Hunter agreement, the men set about buying food, bedrolls, digging tools and dynamite, high-powered rifles and pistols, snake-bite kits and two pack mules for the trip. They wanted to keep their hunting trip a secret, so they bought their supplies in Oklahoma City. After renting a large truck in which they packed the mules and supplies, the men formed a caravan with the truck as lead vehicle. They left at lunch-time on Saturday, April 23, 1966, driving straight through to Arizona.

On Sunday afternoon, Magill and company arrived at their destination, the trailhead at Peralta Canyon, almost three miles south of Bluff Spring Mountain. After setting up what they called the Peralta One camp, the men quickly got a taste of life in the Sonoran desert. One man almost put his sleeping bag on a nest of poisonous centipedes. When the group set off to hunt gold on Monday morning, the temperature was already above 90 degrees.

Magill and three others left camp that morning and by midday they were halfway up Bluff Spring Mountain. A man ahead of the rest fell, landing on a small plateau. The others caught up, and after finding their partner uninjured, decided to take a much needed rest. It was then that one of the men spied a cave opening to a tunnel—a vital clue on the map. The map showed the Sombrero mine directly above a tunnel on the side of a mountain. Only one barrier lay between the men and the gold, a sheer wall of solid rock. The men knew they could not climb to the gold mine, so they decided to use a helicopter that would drop them off on top of the mountain. Suddenly, they heard a blast and were in the middle of a pebble storm.

Darting down the mountain, Magill came across Al Morrow, the Samaritan of Superstition Mountain. Morrow approached Magill apologizing for his error. He had no idea the men were on the mountain. Morrow invited everyone to his cabin for a cup of coffee and an explanation. Half of the men believed the blasting an accident, but the other half thought Morrow set off the dynamite on purpose. He wanted to scare them away from the area. Because of Morrow's mistake, Magill knew they were hunting in the right spot. Old Snowbeard's mysterious gold mine had to be above the tunnel they found earlier.

As soon as they could, Magill and crew moved camp to the top of Bluff Spring Mountain. With the use of a helicopter, they dropped their supplies and scurried to the area where they found the tunnel. It took a few days, but Magill's group found the spot marked by an "X" on the map, the Lost Dutchman Gold Mine. The next step, file a mining claim and dig up the gold.

On Thursday, May 5, 1966, Magill and company filed six claims on the Dutchman mine. Eleven days later, the six partners, plus one more for money, formed the Lost Dutchman Exploration Company. They were now ready to become millionaires.

The story broke. Newspaper reporters rushed to the area. A Tucson radio station hounded Magill to let them do a show from the site of the Lost Dutchman Mine. Magill finally agreed. The radio station had Sidney Brinkerhoff, a member of the Arizona Pioneer's Historical Society, play the Lost Dutchman expert. Brinkerhoff examined Magill's case clue by clue. Finally, after careful study, Brinkerhoff ended the radio show by saying Magill and company were the closest in matching clues. "If in the weeks ahead," Brinkerhoff said, "they are to hit pay dirt, it will be because they have gone at this project with a conscientious and scientific approach."

But the Lost Dutchman Exploration Company lived a short life. Not long after the radio show, the company had problems paying bills. Two of the men working at the mine drank some bad water, which put them in the hospital for a couple of days. Other mishaps occurred and the cost of time and tools became too much to bear. Company members started selling their claims giving up on the idea of every finding Old Snowbeard's gold.

The Oklahoma Securities Commission was the one to put an end to the Lost Dutchman Exploration Company on June 7, 1967. They issued a Cease and Desist Order against the company. No one had thought to register with the State for a license to sell stock. When the men sold their mining claims, they were selling stock in the company and breaking the law.

Magill refused to give up the case. He returned to the Superstitions several times during 1967, frantically searching for the gold. As his money ran out, so did his dream of finding Old Snowbeard's gold. By the end of the year, after spending hundreds of dollars and losing his friends, Magill quit the case. He returned to Oklahoma City and his detective business.

Although Magill stopped hunting Old Snowbeard's gold, others picked up his quest. Claims of finding the Lost Dutchman continued to make local news in the 1970s. In the 1980s, even a psychic said he found the Lost Dutchman by using his powers. But out of all the people claiming to have found the mine, not one could come up with the same rich gold ore Waltz bought supplies with way back in 1884.

Then in December of 1983, Walter Gassler returned to Arizona to make his claim on Old Snowbeard's gold. The first thing Gassler did was find two local Dutchman Hunters and ask for help. The men were Robert Corbin, then Arizona's Attorney General, and Tom Kollenborn, a geologist and historian. Gassler, in his mid-eighties, told Kollenborn and Corbin he knew where Waltz hid his gold. Gassler also told the men to hurry, they had less than a month to find the mine and make a claim. The Wilderness Act of 1964 would prevent the filing of new mining claims in the Superstitions as of midnight, December 31, 1983. Both Kollenborn and Corbin could not help. Gassler went after the gold himself.

In May of 1984, hikers found Walter Gassler's body near Charleybois Spring on the east side of the Superstitions. The Coroner said Gassler died from a heart attack, but just as in the case of Adolph Ruth, not everyone agrees with the Corner. The week after they found his body, a man claiming to be Gassler's son showed up at Kollenborn's front door. The man asked for his father's diary and showed Kollenborn some gold ore. Kollenborn was the one to tell Corbin that the ore he saw and the gold from under Waltz's deathbed were almost identical. When Gassler's real son later asked for a copy of his father's diary, Kollenborn wondered who the stranger with Waltz's gold could be. Did the mysterious man kill Gassler? Did Gassler find the Lost Dutchman? We may never know, the stranger vanished.

The Wilderness Act that rushed Gassler into the Superstitions gave the United States Forest Service the tools they needed to preserve Old Snowbeard's prospecting grounds. Besides saying no to new mining claims, the Act bans motorized vehicles and limits camping to less than fourteen days in a row. These rules help protect the natural desert wilderness so that visitors can enjoy a hike in the same place Waltz walked. In the Superstition Wilderness, Forest Rangers maintain hiking trails. The Treasure Loop, Prospector's View, Jacob's Crosscut, Siphon Draw and Discovery trails make hunting Old Snowbeard's gold an easier task. But even today, with over a century's worth of searching, no one knows for sure where Old Snowbeard got his gold. Will someone ever find Waltz's mysterious gold mine?

9

END OF A CENTURY

Even today, over a century since his death, Waltz and his gold are still making history. A trip to Apache Junction for the annual Lost Dutchman Days shows how much the mystery of Old Snowbeard's gold has grown.

On Saturday morning, February 27, 1999, people start gathering along the Apache Trail in the center of Apache Junction. Some men dressed in old cavalry uniforms are on horseback.

HUNTING OLD SNOWBEARD'S GOLD

    Others are sitting in the back of a covered wagon drawn by horses. A Deputy Sheriff riding a horse talks with a fellow Officer on an ATV. United States Marines arrive and park a small red pickup along the east curb. In the pickup is a six-foot stuffed bear wearing a uniform. Rows of lounge chairs begin lining the streets with grandparents hugging children in their laps. Parents adjust strollers with babies and wave older kids to the front of the curb. The parade is about to begin—it is almost nine o'clock.

    Although the parade is exciting, a 9-year-old boy looks to the north hoping to see the Ferris wheel he rode the day before. A carnival with rides, display booths and Senior Pro Rodeo moves into the Event Center every year for the three day Lost Dutchman Days festival. For the past thirty-five years the city of Apache Junction and Chamber of Commerce have celebrated the mystery of Old Snowbeard's gold.

    Almost four miles north of the carnival grounds is a place open year round, the Goldfield Ghost Town.

END OF A CENTURY

In the heart of Goldfield, among rustic buildings lining Main Street is the Superstition Mountain Lost Dutchman Museum. Waltz himself might feel comfortable drinking a cold sarsaparilla in the Mammoth Saloon looking across at the Livery Stable. He may find the general store, Sheriff's office and Narrow Gauge Railroad familiar. But the helicopter sitting on a cement pad next to the train station would definitely confuse him. Waltz could tour the town on the train or in a horse drawn carriage. Better yet, he could travel trails made for jeep tours. Maybe he could find some forgotten gold while on a tour of the Mammoth Mine, or ask Ron Feldman to take him to his gold in the Superstitions.

Feldman would jump at the chance to take Old Snowbeard to his secret gold mine. Dressed in jeans, cotton shirt, cowboy boots and black hat, Feldman appears to be an old ranch hand. He runs the Livery Stable in Goldfield and owns the oldest pack station in the Superstitions, the OK Corral. Feldman would even know what Waltz needed for a prospecting trip—he is also a Dutchman Hunter.

Feldman started hunting Old Snowbeard's gold when he was twenty years old, back in 1965. As a child, he had heard of the Lost Dutchman, but "it was a kid kind of thing."

After seeing a television show about the Lost Dutchman, Feldman started seriously hunting for Waltz's gold.

Just like Old Snowbeard, Feldman hunts the lost mine by himself. A typical prospecting trip for Feldman is usually a day or two. Feldman once stayed almost three months straight in the mountains.

Ask Feldman why he still searches after all this time and he tells you about the modern day pioneers. "Certain people were the first people to mount the wagons, mount the horses and head their families out west. That's all gone now. So, how do you do it today? Well, part of the way you do it is treasure hunting. You go back in time, search for these things, so you're living in the part of the history at that time. You're living like they did, off the land so to speak, or off the back of a horse and you are hunting something that is an adventure itself. You're kind of the modern day pioneer and not everybody has that glimmer."

Feldman believes that Old Snowbeard's gold is still missing because of an earthquake that rocked the area on May 3, 1887. It changed the Superstitions forever. The soldiers at Fort McDowell, 30 miles east of Phoenix, said they saw a huge cloud of dust rising from the desert floor.

The shaking mountains caused the dust cloud. Boulders came crashing down and loose slabs of volcanic rock shifted into new positions. According to Feldman, this is why nobody can find the mine, the earthquake buried Old Snowbeard's gold. In addition, any map or clue leading to the mine became useless; they no longer matched the terrain.

By matching clues to what the Superstitions must have looked like before the earthquake, Feldman believes he knows where Waltz hid his gold. Feldman will not say where he thinks the Lost Dutchman Mine is, but he does say it will take time and tons of digging to find it.

Not everyone agrees with Feldman. From the Lost Dutchman State Park, located five miles north of Apache Junction, John Wilburn takes a group of people once a year to what he says is Waltz's gold mine. This year, 1999 is his last tour, the Bureau of Land Management will close the area to public access. A darn shame too, he weaves quite a case when he gives his annual tour during the Lost Dutchman Days.

"Here's the little north-trending gulch Waltz referred to right through here," he tells a crowd standing near the Bulldog Mine.

"This is a gulch running north and south and the mine was said to have been high above the gulch and well concealed by brush. Well, of course, they've stripped all the brush away now over the years, but at one time it was extremely brushy here."

Wilburn addresses the high peak so often referred to in the Lost Dutchman Gold Mine legend. Wilburn tells people that Waltz "never said Weaver's Needle, obviously because there's no gold there, no mines. The peak he was talking about was Bulldog Peak."

Another Lost Dutchman clue Wilburn talks about is the late shadow of the high peak. "Some say that the late shadow of the peak fell right across the ledge of gold. Well, around April 17 and in August, the shadow of Bulldog Peak—I've been over here—falls exactly across the Stope over there." The Stope Wilburn points to is the opening of the Bulldog Mine.

So many clues and even more theories. Did the mine ever exist? Will anyone ever find the gold? Perhaps in the next century someone will solve the mystery, where did Old Snowbeard get his gold?

10

THE NEXT CENTURY

This year at the 48th Annual Lost Dutchman Days, an additional celebration is in the works—Arizona's 100th Anniversary. On February 14, 1912, the Arizona Territory became the forty-eighth State of the Union. To help with the Centennial celebration, Theodore Roosevelt, the twenty-sixth President of the United States and George W.P. Hunt, Arizona's first Governor will join Old Snowbeard. They are in town to dedicate three monuments at the Superstition Mountain Museum on Saturday, February 25, 2012. The monuments have original concrete blocks from the Theodore Roosevelt Dam. Completed in 1911, the dam prevents another flood like the one that almost washed Waltz away back in 1891. A crew had to build a road just to get equipment and supplies to the construction site. The road snakes north 60 miles through mountain canyons from Apache Junction to Roosevelt lake. Opened to travelers in 1905, the road is nicknamed the Apache Trail.

The dedication ceremony of the three monuments celebrates the end of one hundred years and marks the next century for the State of Arizona, the Theodore Roosevelt Dam and the Apache Trail.

After the ceremony, the actors portraying the legendary figures will wander over to Goldfield Ghost Town. By now, Old Snowbeard's ghost should be familiar with the town; it hasn't changed much since 1999. The OK Corral owned by Ron Feldman is still there and John Wilburn has a clear shot of the Bulldog Mine west of town. The Museum is different. Now called the Goldfield Museum, most exhibits about Waltz and his gold are gone. They reside in the Superstition Mountain Museum, which opened in December 2003.

THE NEXT CENTURY

The museum located south of Goldfield and across the Apache Trail has more than Lost Dutchman history to see. Waltz might enjoy the wildlife display, or the military uniforms and Native American artifacts. The Elvis Memorial Chapel and Audie Murphy Barn will probably confuse Old Snowbeard taking a stroll outside. Even the twenty-stamp ore crusher could cause him to shake his head in surprise. After all, it was the newest machine used for gold mining back in the 1800s. Instead of using a pick to break the gold free from the ore, the machine smashes the ore.

Maybe Waltz will wander the twelve-acre site until he comes across a familiar trail leading him back into the Superstition Mountains. Instead of his gold mine, Old Snowbeard may come across the skeleton of a lost Dutchman Hunter.

A man from Denver by the name of Jesse Capen decided to hunt Waltz's gold on his own in December 2009. Obsessed with the Lost Dutchman, Jesse took a month vacation from his job as a bellhop in a downtown Denver hotel. At the age of 35, Jesse said goodbye to his Mom and made his final hunting trip to the Superstitions. His whereabouts are still unknown today.

The tools Jesse used to search for gold could overwhelm Old Snowbeard. Besides hundreds of books and maps, Capen used his computer and the World Wide Web.

A quick Internet search on the Lost Dutchman Gold Mine results in hundreds of Web sites ranging from a group of Dutchman Hunters selling books, tapes, CDs and maps to an article claiming the author found the mine using a satellite mapping service. Then again, the musical ring tone of a cellular phone will probably frighten Old Snowbeard enough to take his burro and hightail it out of the area. That could be the reason why three Utah men did not bring their phones when they ventured into the Superstitions on July 6, 2010. The *Apache Junction Gold Canyon News* for the week of July 19, 2010 had a front-page story headlined:

> RESCUERS SEARCH FOR 3 UTAH HIKERS
> TREASURE HUNTERS TRIED TO BRAVE THE INTENSE SUMMER HEAT.

The men, Curtis Merworth, Ardean Charles and Malcolm Meeks parked their vehicle at the First Water trailhead on the north side of the

Superstitions and hiked into the wilderness hunting Old Snowbeard's gold. Curtis was the lead Dutchman Hunter; he tried finding the gold in 2009 but ended up getting lost. He and two other men were lucky that time, they were found alive. This time, a year later, Merworth and his men were not so lucky. The Digital Journal posted an article on July 20, 2010 entitled:

> Search called off for missing Utah treasure hunters.

The search started on Sunday, July 11 with four helicopters, a small airplane using thermal imaging equipment and dozens of Deputies on foot and horseback. There was a heat wave that summer, temperatures hung around 116°F. The Maricopa County Sheriff's Department ended their search efforts the following Sunday, July 18, 2010. A group of volunteers known as the Superstition Search and Rescue Team picked up the efforts trying to find the missing Utah Dutchman Hunters for five more months. Besides an empty car at the First Water trailhead, there was no other sign of the men. It was as if the Thundergod turned them into stone.

Then, on January 5, 2011, a fellow prospector found two of the lost Utah Dutchman Hunters' bodies.

Two miles off the First Water trailhead, sat a pair of fully clothed skeletons on a slab of volcanic rocks at the base of Yellow Peak. There were umbrellas nearby too, probably used for shelter from the scorching sun. What killed them was the outdoor oven they sat on. Since dark clothes retain the Sun's heat, people usually wear light colored clothes in summer months. The surface heat of the black rocks had to be similar to the top of a charcoal grill fired up and ready for cooking.

The skeleton of the last lost Utah Dutchman Hunter showed up on January 13, 2011. The Superstition Search and Rescue Team saw what looked to be some bones not far from where the other two skeletons laid. They had to make a return trip on January 15 to get close enough to see that the bones were human. It took the use of a Maricopa County Rescue Helicopter to pick up the remains.

Is the risk of dehydration and death really worth finding the Lost Dutchman Gold Mine? Most of today's Prospectors will shout a resounding, "Yes!"

On February 7, 2012, an ounce of gold sold for $1,746 according to Goldprice™. Quite an increase from when President Roosevelt set the price at $35 an ounce in 1934. Also posted was a note which read: "Gold Price Has Been on a Short Term Correction for the Last Three Days but Wants to Climb Higher."

Good news for prospectors—bad news for search and rescue teams, especially those out in the summer heat looking for inexperienced Dutchman Hunters.

Although prospectors are not flocking to the Superstitions as they did in the 1930s, their death toll continues to rise. Not everyone has the horse sense to pack enough supplies and plenty of water when hunting Old Snowbeard's gold. Some even know how to avoid the summer heat. Venturing into the Superstitions can be dangerous at any time of the year. There are wild mountain lions as well as crazed prospectors who will do anything to protect their territory. Mining for gold in the Superstition Wilderness Area is against the law unless a prospector had a claim filed before midnight December 31, 1983. The fear of being arrested does not stop outlaw prospectors, some of them are as well armed as Ed Piper and Celeste Maria Jones. An unwitting Dutchman Hunter might be mistaken for a claim jumper and end up with a hole in his head like Adolph Ruth.

Nowadays, not everyone needs to risk their lives hunting Old Snowbeard's gold. Enjoying the western adventure can be done at a computer using satellite maps and Internet Web sites, in a chair sorting through pages of books and copies of maps, or on foot hiking paths in the Lost Dutchman State Park.

Jim Bark, the one who first called it the Lost Dutchman said, "Someone, someday will fit the parts together more successfully than we have done. Good luck to him [or her]."

Not everyone is as lucky as Waltz—he came out of the Superstitions alive. Despite the danger, people will continue hunting Old Snowbeard's gold making history as they go adding tales to the legend of the Lost Dutchman Gold Mine.

THINGS AS THEY HAPPENED

1810	Jacob Waltz is born.
1826	North Carolina has their first gold rush.
1828	Northern Georgia has their first gold rush.
1839	Waltz arrived in America, either New York or Baltimore.
1848	February 2, the signing of the Mexican-American War Treaty makes the legendary Peralta Sombrero Mine property of the United States.
1848	September 12, Waltz signs a Letter of Intention to become a citizen of the United States in Natchez, Mississippi.
1860	Census taken by Azusa Township, County of Los Angeles lists Waltz as a day laborer working at a gold mine.
1861	July 19, Waltz becomes a citizen of the United States.

1863	September 21, Waltz files the Gross Lode mining claim in Prescott, Arizona.
1864	In May, the Prescott Postmaster lists Waltz as a miner from Germany, two years in the Territory.
1864	September 14, Waltz files the Big Rebel mining claim in Prescott, Arizona.
1865	According to legend, in the fall, Doctor Abram Thorne becomes the first white man to see Waltz's gold.
1865	December 27, Waltz files the General Grant Lode mining claim in Prescott, Arizona.
1868	March or April, Waltz moves from Prescott almost 107 miles south to Phoenix, Arizona.
1870	August 30, the Federal Census for the Territory of Arizona, Yavapai County lists Waltz as a 60-year-old farmer.
1872	March 21, Waltz files an Affidavit of Claim Jumping in the Pinal County Courthouse.
1873	People start seeing Waltz roaming the Superstition Wilderness and selling gold in Florence, Arizona.
1875	Waltz pays taxes in Phoenix.
1876	Waltz registers to vote in Phoenix.
1877	Waltz pays taxes in Phoenix.

1877	According to Brownie Holmes, this is the year Waltz found his gold mine.
1878	August 8, Waltz signs his land and property over to his neighbor Andrew Starar in return for care during an illness.
1882	Waltz registers to vote in Phoenix.
1884	Eyewitness sees Old Snowbeard buying supplies with a pouch of gold ore.
1884	June 18, an article about a man being shot at Waltz's ranch appears in the *Arizona Gazette*.
1886	Waltz registers to vote in Phoenix.
1887	May 3, an earthquake rocks the Superstitions and, according to some, buries Waltz's gold mine.
1888	Dick Holmes meets Waltz in Phoenix for the first time.
1890	December, Waltz tells Julia Thomas and Rhinehart "Reiney" Petrasch about his secret gold mine while enjoying a meal at his place.
1891	February 19, the Salt River floods and washes part of Phoenix away.
1891	March, Waltz plans to take Thomas and Reiney to his secret gold mine when the weather is good for camping.
1891	October 25, Waltz dies in the one-room adobe behind Thomas' shop in Phoenix.

1891	October 26, the day of Waltz's funeral and the gold under his bed is missing.
1892	January or February, Dick Holmes sells some of Waltz's gold and he and Gideon Roberts starts hunting Old Snowbeard's gold.
1892	February or March, Gideon Roberts dies.
1892	July 10, Thomas sells her store in Phoenix and prepares to find Waltz's gold mine.
1892	August 11, Thomas and the Petrasch brothers leave Phoenix in search for Waltz's gold mine.
1892	August 27, the article entitled "A Queer Quest" appears in the *Arizona Daily Gazette*.
1894	November 17, *Phoenix Saturday Review* prints an article about the Lost Dutchman Gold Mine.
1895	August 24, *Phoenix Saturday Review* prints another article about the Lost Dutchman Gold Mine.
1901	September 28, a Prescott, Arizona, newspaper prints the first article about Waltz finding the Peralta's *El Sombrero* mine.
1905	The Mesa-Roosevelt road is complete, later renamed the Apache Trail.
1908	At the age of sixteen, Brownie Holmes joins his father to search for Waltz's gold mine.

1911	March, President Theodore Roosevelt dedicates the Theodore Roosevelt Dam.
1912	February 14, Arizona becomes the forty-eighth State of the Union.
1917	December 22, Julia Thomas dies.
1919	Adolph Ruth falls from a ledge breaking his hip hunting a Peralta mine in California.
1931	In the Spring, Ruth retires from his job.
1931	May 4, Ruth leaves Washington, DC with a friend to hunt the Lost Dutchman Gold Mine.
1931	June 13, Ruth sets up camp by Willow Spring and begins hunting Old Snowbeard's gold.
1931	June 18, a posse starts searching for Ruth.
1931	August 1, after forty-five days of searching, the Pinal and Maricopa County Sheriff Departments presume Ruth dead calling off the search.
1931	December 13, the Arizona Republic reports the finding of Ruth's skull.
1932	January 8, Tex Barkley and a Deputy Sheriff find Ruth's skeleton in West Boulder Canyon.
1932	Thomas Wiggins creates a gold rush to Superior when he thought he found Old Snowbeard's gold.

1932	Walter Gassler starts his hunt for Waltz's gold after reading an article about the Lost Dutchman in the *Oakland Tribune*.
1934	President Roosevelt sets gold prices at $35 an ounce.
1934	Gassler pitches a tent next to an empty drug store and moves to Apache Junction, Arizona.
1934	A Pawtucket, Rhode Island man sends a letter to the Phoenix Chamber of Commerce telling them where to find the Lost Dutchman Gold Mine.
1937	September 3, Barry Storm registers his first mining claim in the Superstitions.
1943	February 4, Rhinehart "Reiney" Petrasch ends his life with a shotgun.
1943	March 17, Storm files another mining claim in the Superstitions.
1946	April, Ludwig Rosecrans, the Resident Philosopher, finds some surface gold and moves into the Superstitions.
1949	Al Morrow, the Samaritan of Superstition Mountain moves to the area by setting up a six-by-eight foot tent in Needle Canyon.
1949	The movie, *Lust for Gold*, based on one of Storm's books, opens in theaters.
1949	December 2, Celeste Maria Jones makes her first mining claim

	near Weaver's Needle calling it Peralta Mines.
1952	Edgar "Ed" Piper builds a shelter in East Boulder Canyon, moves in and plants fruit trees.
1952	One of Rosecrans' mining claims rewards him with sixteen tons of gold ore.
1953	November 23, Hermann Petrasch dies alone in his shack along Queen Creek.
1954	November 15, Jones files a second mining claim near Weaver's Needle calling it Bluff Springs.
1956	February 9, Piper files his first mining claim near Weaver's Needle calling it the Thing Number One.
1958	November 24, Jones files her third mining claim near Weaver's Needle calling it Black Mesa.
1958	Throughout the year, Piper files four more mining claims near Weaver's Needle calling them the Thing Number Two, Three, Four and Five.
1959	January, Robert Sikorsky joins Jones' camp as the gold expert.
1959	Early April, Robert Sikorsky quits after being shot at.
1959	November 11, Piper kills Robert St. Marie in self-defense.
1959	November 25, Ralph Thomas, a friend of Jones, kills Lavern Rowlee in self-defense.
1960	January 1, the *Apache Sentinel* reports that Justice of the Peace

	Normal L. Teason tries to stop Jones and Piper from feuding by taking away their rifles.
1960	October 23, hikers find the body of Franz Harrier, an Australian exchange student, in the Superstitions.
1961	March 21, a hiker finds the body of Walter J. Mowry, a Dutchman Hunter from Denver, Colorado.
1961	Around November, hikers find the body of Charles Bohen, a Dutchman Hunter from Salt Lake City, Utah.
1962	June 24, a friend finds Piper extremely sick at his camp in the Superstitions. They use a helicopter to fly him to a hospital in Florence, Arizona.
1962	August 13, Edgar "Ed" Piper dies.
1963	March 26, Vance Bacon, who worked for Jones, fell to his death while dangling on a rope hanging from the side of Weaver's Needle.
1963	Shortly after the death of Bacon, the men working for Celeste Maria Jones quit and she quietly disappears from the Superstition Wilderness.

1963	The Pinal County Sheriff issues a warning telling people to stay away from the Superstitions; too many people have died while hunting Old Snowbeard's gold.
1964	Glenn Magill, a private detective, begins his search for the Lost Dutchman Gold Mine.
1964	December, Magill flies over the Superstitions in a helicopter and uses aerial photography as a modern method of prospecting.
1965	March, Magill makes another trip into the Superstitions, this time on foot and with a friend.
1965	Ron Feldman begins his hunt for the Lost Dutchman Gold Mine.
1966	January 5, Magill receives traced-copies of three maps once belonging to Adolph Ruth.
1966	April, Magill and his Spanish speaking wife decipher clues behind the maps.
1966	April 23, Magill and company leave Oklahoma City at noon for the Superstition Wilderness in Arizona. They begin hunting Old

	Snowbeard's gold on Monday, April 25.
1966	May 5, Magill and company file six claims on the Dutchman mine.
1966	May 16, Magill and six other men form the Lost Dutchman Exploration Company.
1967	June 7, the Oklahoma Securities Commission issues a Cease and Desist Order against the Lost Dutchman Exploration Company.
1967	December, Magill quits hunting Old Snowbeard's gold and returns to his private detective business in Oklahoma.
1970	September 9, a Sheriff Deputy finds the body of Albert Morrow, the Samaritan of the Superstitions under a boulder near his camp.
1980	A psyche claims to have found the Lost Dutchman by using his powers.
1980	April 11, George "Brownie" Holmes dies.
1983	December, Gassler returns to hunt the Lost Dutchman.
1983	December 31, the Wilderness Act of 1964 stops the claiming of new gold mines in the Superstitions as of midnight.
1984	May, hikers find Walter Gassler's body near Charleybois Spring.
1986	April 7, Ludwig Rosecrans, the Resident Philosopher, dies.

1996	The Theodore Roosevelt Dam is modernized raising the water level capacity.
1999	February 26, 27 and 28, the City of Apache Junction and Chamber of Commerce hold the 35th annual Lost Dutchman Days festival.
2003	December, the Superstition Mountain Museum opens.
2009	December, Jesse Capen disappears hunting the Lost Dutchman.
2010	July 6, Curtis Merworth, Ardean Charles and Malcom Meeks from Utah hike into the Superstitions hunting Old Snowbeard's gold.
2010	July 11, Maricopa County Search and Rescue Team seek the three missing Utah Dutchman Hunters.
2010	July 18, Maricopa County Sheriff's Department ends their search efforts for the lost Utah Dutchman Hunters.
2011	January 5, the skeletons of two lost Utah Dutchman Hunters are found by a fellow prospector.
2011	January 13, Superstition Search and Rescue Team spy what they think are bones.

2011	January 15, the skeletal remains of the third missing Utah Dutchman Hunter are removed by helicopter.
2012	February 7, Goldprice™ shows an ounce of gold at $1,746 with headline stating prices may increase.
2012	February 24, 25 and 26, the City of Apache Junction and Chamber of Commerce hold the 48th Annual Lost Dutchman Days festival.
2012	February 25, dedication of Centennial Monuments at the Superstition Mountain Museum.

LIST OF FURTHER EXPLORING

If you want to learn more about Old Snowbeard and his mysterious gold, below are some places you might find worth writing to or exploring on the Internet.

Apache Junction Chamber of Commerce
567 West Apache Trail, Apache Junction, Arizona 85220
Web Address: ApacheJunctionCOC.com

Apache Junction Public Library
1177 North Idaho Road, Apache Junction, Arizona 85119
Web Address: www.AJPL.org

Arizona Historical Society
Southern Arizona Division, Library and Archives
949 East Second Street, Tucson, Arizona 85719
Web Address: www.ArizonaHistoricalSociety.org

Goldfield Ghost Town
4650 North Mammoth Mine Road, Goldfield, Arizona 85219
Web Address: www.GoldfieldGhostTown.com

Lost Dutchman Days
Web Address: www.LostDutchmanDays.org

Lost Dutchman State Park
6109 North Apache Trail, Apache Junction, Arizona 85119
Web Address: AZStateParks.com/Parks/LODU

Pinal County Historical Society and Museum
715 South Main Street, Florence, Arizona 85232
Web Address: PinalCountyHistoricalSociety.Webs.Com

Superstition Mountain Historical Society and Museum
4087 North Apache Trail, Apache Junction, Arizona 85119
Web Address: www.SuperstitionMountainMuseum.org

Tom Kollenborn Chronicles
Web Address: SuperstitionMountainTomKollenborn.blogspot.com

BIBLIOGRAPHY

"A Mythical Mine." *Saturday Review* 17 November 1894: 1. Print.
"A Queer Quest." *Arizona Daily Gazette* 27 August 1892: 4. Print.
"After the High Tide." *Phoenix Daily Herald* 20 February 1891: 3. Print.
America A to Z: People, Customs, and Culture. Pleasantville: Reader's Digest Association, 1997. Print.
"Arizona Atlas and Gazetteer." Freeport: DeLorme, 1996. Print.
Arnold, Oren. *Ghost Gold.* 3rd. San Antonio: Naylor, 1960. Print.
—. *Hidden Treasure in the Wild West.* New York: Abelard-Schuman Ltd., 1966. Print.
Barron, Alicia E. "Mother of Group Leader in Lost Dutchman Gold Mission Talks to 3TV." 14 July 2010. *AZFamily.com.* KTVK, Inc. Web. September 16 2010. <http://www.azfamily.com/news/local/Mother-of-group-leader-among-missing-treasure-hunters-talks-to-3TV-98479099,html>.
Bernauw, Patrick. "The Lost Dutchman Gold Mine Found?" 20 November 2009. *Unexplained Mysteries.* Web. 8 February 2012. <http://www.unexplained-mysteries.com/column.php?id=169267>.
Black, Harry G. *The Lost Dutchman Mine: A Short Story of a Tall Tale.* Boston: Branden, 1975. Print.
Blair, Robert. *Tales of the Superstitions: The Origins of the Lost Dutchman Legend.* Tempe: Arizona Historical Foundation, 1975. Print.
Brooks, Helen. "Reporter Fascinated by Trip into Superstitions." *Apache Sentinel* 29 September 1961: sec. 1: 6. Print.

Carlson, Jack and Elizabeth Stewart. *Hiker's Guide to the Superstition Wilderness: With History and Legends of Arizona's Lost Dutchman Gold Mine*. Tempe: Clear Creek, 1995. Print.

Cizmar, Martin. "Jesse Capen Went Searching for Lost Dutchman Gold. Now They're Searching for Him." 3 June 2010. *www.westword.com*. Web. 8 February 2012. <http://www.westword.com/content/printVersion/1491461>.

"Colorado Man Disappears in Search for Gold Mine." 17 January 2010. *KVOA.com*. Web. 2012 February 2010. <http://kvoa.com/news/colorado-man-disappears-in-search-for-gold-mine>.

Cooper, B. Thomas. "Search Called Off for Missing Utah Treasure Hunters." 20 July 2010. *Digital Journal*. Web. 16 September 2010. <http://www.digitaljournal.com/print/article/294911>.

—. "Temperatures Approach 116 as Search for Lost Hikers Continues." 15 July 2010. *Digital Journal*. Web. 16 September 2010.

Corbin, Helen. *The Curse of the Dutchman's Gold: The True Story of Arizona's Most Cryptic Mine*. Phoenix: Foxwest, 1990. Print.

"Dutch Jacob's Mine." *Saturday Review* 25 August 1895: 1-2. Print.

Ely, Sims. *The Lost Dutchman Mine*. New York: William Morrow and Company, 1960. Print.

Events - Theodore Roosevelt Visits the Museum. 10 January 2012. Web. 7 February 2012. <http://www.superstitionmountainmuseum.org/events/details/87-theodore-roosevelt-visits-the-museum>.

Facts About Gold. n.d. Web. 1999 March 9. <http://www.goldinstitute.com/history.htm>.

Feldman, Ron. Interview. Eleanor Mell. 27 February 1999. Personal interview.

"Foul Murder." *Arizona Gazette* 18 June 1884, Daily ed.: 3. Print.

Fraser, Jay. *Lost Dutchman Mine Discoveries and a History of Arizona Mining*. Tucson: Trail to Yesterday, 1988. Print.

Fuoco-Karasinski, Christina. "Rescuers Seach for 3 Utah Hikers." 19 July 2010. *Apache Junction Gold Canyon News*. www.ajnews.com. Web. 7 February 2012. <http://ajnews.com/vol14/071910/pdfs/0719_com-AJNW_A1.pdf>.

Gardner, Earle Stanley. *Hunting Lost Mines by Helicopter*. New York: William Morrow and Company, 1965. Print.

Garman, Robert L. *Mystery Gold of the Superstitions*. Mesa: Lane Print & Pub, 1975. Print.

BIBLIOGRAPHY

Gassler, Walter. *The Lost Peralta-Dutchman Mine*. Apache Junction: Superstition Mountain Historical Society Rare Book Reprint, 1983. Print.

Gentry, Curt. *The Killer Mountains, A Search for the Legendary Lost Dutchman Mine*. New York: New American Library, 1968. Print.

Hall, Sharlot M. "Lost Mines: Romance of the Mines: Lost Dutchman of the Superstition Mountains." *Yavapai* April 1919: 17. Print.

"Happy Birthday! Arizona, 100 Years—February 14, 2012." 6 February 2012. *Apache Junction Gold Canyon News*. www.ajnews.com. Web. 20 February 2012. <http://ajnews.com/vol16/020612/0206_com_AJNW_A1.pdf>.

"Hearing for Piper Delayed to June 28." *Apache Sentinel* 22 June 1962: 1. Print.

"Hiking Trails, Lost Dutchman State Park." Apache Junction: Arizona State Parks, 27 February 1999. Print.

"History." n.d. *FRBSF Currency Exhibit: Historical Context: Metal Standards*. Web. 17 September 1999. <http://www.frbsf.org/currency/metal/history/text1.html>.

Holmes, George Brownie. *Story of the Lost Dutchman*. Apache Junction: Superstition Mountain Historical Society Rare Book Reprint, 1990. Print.

Jennings, Gary. *The Treasures of the Superstition Mountains*. New York: WW Norton and Company, Inc, 1973. Print.

"Killer Acquitted." *Apache Sentinel* 4 December 1959: 1. Print.

Kollenborn, Thomas J. and James A. Swanson. *History of Apache Junction*. Apache Junction: That Other Printer, 1990. Print.

Kollenborn, Tom. "A Deadly Vision." 28 February 2011. *Apache Junction Gold Canyon News*. www.ajnews.com. Web. 8 February 2012. <http://www.ajnews.com/vol15/022811/pdfs/0228_com_AJNW_A4.pdf>.

—. "Arizona's Apache Trail." 16 January 2012. *Apache Junction Gold Canyon News*. www.ajnews.com. Web. 2012 February 2. <http://ajnews.com/vol16/011612/0116_com_AJNW_A1.pdf>.

Kollenborn, Tom and the Superstition Mountain Historical Society. "The Lost Dutchman Mine: History and Bibliography." n.d. *Text and Bibliography of Lost Dutchman's Mine*. Web. 1998 April 30. <http://ajnet.ci.apache-jct.az.s/ldm.htm>.

Lehman, Clarice. "Dr. Thorne's Lost Mine." *Arizona Highways* April 1999: 25-28. Print.

Lost Dutchman Days. n.d. Web. 30 January 2012. <http://www.lostdutchmandays.org>.

Lost Dutchman State Park. n.d. Arizona State Parks. Web. 20 February 2012. <http://www.pr.state.az.us/parkhtml/dutchman.html>.

"Man's Body Found Near Weaver's Needle." *Arizona Republic* 22 April 1998: sec. B: 1. Print.

MapBlast. n.d. Vicinity Corporation. Web. 17 June 1999. <http://www.mapblast.com>.

"No Title." *Phoenix Daily Herald* 26 October 1891: 3. Print.

Sherlock, Joseph M. *The Fifties - A Brief History.* n.d. Web. 24 March 1999. <http://www.joesherlock.com/fifties.html>.

Sikorsky, Robert. *Quest for the Dutchman's Gold: The 100-Year Mystery.* Phoenix: Golden West, 1991. Print.

Silver and Gold Prices. 7 February 2012. Goldprice.org. Web. 8 February 2012. <http://silver-and-gold-prices.goldprice.org>.

"Skull Believed that of Missing Prospector Found in Mountains." *Arizona Republic* 13 December 1931: 1+. Print.

"Sonoran Desert Naturalist." n.d. *Sonoran Desert Naturalist Home Page.* Web. 17 June 1999. <http://members.aol.com/Melasoma/index.html>.

"State Info: Geography." n.d. *Arizona Guide.* Web. 17 June 1999. <http://www.arizonaguide.com/extras/geography.shtml>.

"Story of Superstition Killings to be Seen by Nation-wide TV Audience." *Apache Sentinel* 1 January 1960: 1. Print.

Superstition Mountain Lost Dutchman Museum. n.d. Web. 7 May 1999. <http://ajnet.ci.apache-jct-az.us/museum1.htm>.

Swanson, James A. and Thomas J. Kollenborn. *Superstition Mountain, A Ride Through Time.* Phoenix: Arrowhead Press, 1981. Print.

"Teddy's Schedule of Appearances." n.d. *Lost Dutchman Days.* Superstition Mountain Promotional Corp. Web. 20 February 2012. <http://www.lostdutchmandays.org/forms/schedule-of-events.pdf>.

"The Legend of Superstition Mountain." *The Magazine Tucson* September 1950: 14+. Print.

"The Lost Dutchman." *Newsweek* 18 June 1962: 29. Print.

"The Mint in U.S. History: Mint Growth and Expansion." n.d. *The US Mint: The Mint in US History.* Web. 17 September 1999. <http://www.usmint.gov/facts/UShistory.cfm>.

"The Pima Indian Legend of the Superstition Mountain." Lost Dutchman State Park, n.d. 1. Print. 27 February 1999.

"The Silver Dollar: The 1800s." n.d. *The U.S. Mint: History of Coin Composition at the U.S. Mint.* Web. 17 September 1999. <http://www.usmint.gov/facts/silver1800.cfm>.

"Theodore Roosevelt Dam." n.d. *SRP: Roosevelt Dam.* Web. 11 February 2012. <http://www.srpnet.com/water/dams/roosevelt.aspx>.

"Tonto National Forest Arizona, Gila and Salt River Meridian." U.S. Department of Agriculture Forest Service, 1991. Print.

Wagoneer, Jay J. *Arizona, Its Place in the United States.* Salt Lake City: Gibbs Smith (Peregrine Smith Book), 1989. Print.

"Welcome to the Lost Dutchman Gold Mine." n.d. *The Lost Dutchman Gold Mine.* Frontier Websmiths. Web. 8 February 2012. <http://www.thelostdutchmangoldmine.com>.

"Well Shaken." *Arizona Gazette* 5 May 1887: 3. Print.

Wilburn, John D. Interview. Eleanor Mell. 27 February 1999. Personal Interview.

—. *Dutchman's Lost Ledge of Gold.* 3rd. [Mesa]: General Business and Industrial Printing, 1995. Print.

INDEX

Apache Trail, 51, 57-59, 66
Adams, J.D., 33
Arizona Cities
    Apache Junction, 21, 33, 40, 43, 51–52, 54, 57, 68, 73-74
    Florence, 3, 8, 64, 70
    Globe, 3, 15
    Phoenix, 1, 3, 7, 9–11, 14, 18, 24, 27, 32–33, 40–42, 45, 53, 64–66, 68
    Prescott, 6–7, 25, 64, 66
    Queen Creek, 15, 69
    Superior, 15, 33, 67
    Tortilla Flat, 3
    Tucson, 1, 26, 48
Bacon, Vance, 43, 70
Bark, Jim, 12, 15, 23, 62
Barkley, Tex, 30–34, 67
Black Top Mesa, 34
Bluff Spring Mountain, 14, 46–48, 69
Bohen, Charles, 44, 70
Bulldog Peak, 54–55
Canyon
    East Boulder, 41–42, 69

West Boulder, 32, 67
Needle, 35, 68
Peralta, 47
Capen, Jesse, 59, 73
claim jumper, 8–9, 61
Crandall, Robert, 43
earthquake, 36, 53–54, 65
Ely, Sims, 11–12, 23
Feldman, Ron, 53–54, 58, 71
Gassler, Walter, 33–35, 49–50, 68, 72
Goldfield Ghost Town, 52–53, 58–59
Gold Lighter, 20–21
Harrier, Franz, 44, 70
Hearst, William Randolph, 23
Hewitt Station, 15
Holmes
    Richard "Dick", 8, 10–11, 17–21, 27, 65–66
    George "Brownie", 17–21, 32, 65–66, 72
Jones, Celeste Maria, 40–45, 61, 68–70
Kollenborn, Tom, 1, 49–50
Lost Dutchman
    Days 51–52, 54, 57, 73–74

Exploration Company, 48–49, 72
State Park, 54, 62
Magill, Glenn, 45–49, 71–72
map
    Peralta's, 26–30, 48
    Ruth's, 32, 34, 71
    sandstone. See Peralta's
    Thomas', 14
Counties
    Adams, 6
    Los Angeles, 6, 63
    Maricopa
        Cemetery, 10
        Rescue Helicopter, 61
        Sheriff, 31, 33, 60, 67, 73
    Pinal,
        Courthouse, 8, 64
        Sheriff, 31, 44–45, 67, 71
    Yavapai, 7, 64
Merworth, Curtis, 59–60, 73
mines
    Bulldog, 3, 54–55, 58
    Mammoth, 3, 53
    Peralta's, See Sombrero
    Sombrero, 25–29, 34, 36, 46, 48, 63, 66
    Vulture, 3, 26
mining claim
    Jones', 40, 68–69
    Magill's, 48–49, 72
    Piper's, 42, 69
    Rosecrans', 35, 69
    Storm's, 35, 68
    Waltz's, 6, 64
    Wiggins', 33
Monuments
    Centennial, 57–58, 74

Dutchman, 36–37
Morrow, Albert Erland, 35–36, 43, 48, 68, 72
Mowry, Walter, 44, 70
Museum
    Goldfield, 58
    Superstition Mountain Lost Dutchman, 53
    Superstition Mountain, 57–59, 73–74
Peralta Family, 25–26, 29, 34
Petrasch,
    Hermann, 12–13, 15, 21, 69
    Rhinehart "Reiney", 9–13, 15–17, 20, 65, 68
Phipps, John, 18
Piper, Edgar "Ed", 40–45, 61, 69–70
priests
    Spanish, 41
    Jesuit, 26
Pulitzer, Joseph, 23
ranch
    Barkley's, 30–33
    Bark's, 23
    Martin, 15
    Waltz's, 7, 9, 65
Resident Philosopher. See Rosencrans, Ludwig
Roberts, Gideon, 18, 20–21, 66
Rosecrans, Ludwig, 35, 68–69, 72
Rowlee, Lavern, 43, 69
Ruth
    Adolph, 29–34, 36, 46, 49, 61, 67, 71
    Erwin, 29–32, 46
Samaritan of Superstition. See Morrow, Albert Erland
Search and Rescue Team
    Maricopa, 61, 73
    Superstition, 60–61, 73

INDEX

Sikorsky, Robert, 40–43, 69
Springs
    Charleybois, 34, 49, 72
    Willow, 30, 67
St. Marie, Robert, 43, 69
Storm, Barry, 35, 68
Teason, Justice of the Peace Norman L., 40, 42–43, 70
Thomas
    Julia, 9–21, 40, 65–67
    Ralph, 43, 69
Thorne, Doctor Abram, 24–25, 64
Thundergod, 24–25, 37, 60

trailhead
    First Water, 59–61
    Peralta Canyon, 47
University of Arizona, School of Mines, 21
Waltz Rock, 36
Waltz's nephew, 19
Weaver's Needle, 14–15, 25, 26, 30–32, 35, 40–43, 54, 69–70
Weiser, Jacob, 26
Wiggins, Thomas, 33, 67
Wilburn, John, 54–55, 58
Wilderness Act, 49–50, 72

Printed in Great Britain
by Amazon